Ornamental Flowering Trees & Shurbs

Ornamental Flowering Trees & Shurbs

— Third Edition —

by
A.D. Webster

BIOTECH
2012
Biotech Books
Delhi - 110 035

ISBN 81-7622-166-X

Published by : **BIOTECH BOOKS**
1123/74, Tri Nagar,
DELHI – 110 035
Phone: 27382765
e-mail: biotechbooks@yahoo.co.in

Showroom : 4762-63/23, Ansari Road, Darya Ganj,
NEW DELHI - 110 002
Phone: 23245578, 23244987

Printed at : **Chawla Offset Printers**
New Delhi – 110 052

PRINTED IN INDIA

PREFACE TO THIRD EDITION

THE second edition of "Hardy Ornamental Flowering Trees and Shrubs" having been sold out, a steady demand for the book necessitates the printing of a third edition.

Advantage has been taken of this reprint to thoroughly revise the work, and include such species as have been introduced since the publication of the first edition. Several useful chapters regarding shrubs—their propagation, planting, and general management—are likewise added, as also the natural order to which each belongs.

A. D. W.

REGENT'S PARK,
1908.

PREFACE TO FIRST EDITION, 1893

This book has been written and is published with the distinct object in view of bringing home to the minds of planters of Hardy Trees and Shrubs, the fact that the monotonous repetition, in at least nine-tenths of our Parks and Gardens, of such Trees as the Elm, the Lime, and the Oak, and such Shrubs as the Cherry Laurel and the Privet, is neither necessary nor desirable. There is quite a host of choice and beautiful flowering species, which, though at present not generally known are yet perfectly hardy, of the simplest culture, and equally well adapted for the ornamentation of our Public and Private Parks and Gardens.

Of late years, with the marked decline in the cultivation of Coniferous Trees, many of which are ill adapted for the climate of this country, the interest in our lovely flowering Trees and Shrubs has been greatly revived. This fact has been well exemplified in the numerous inquiries after these subjects, and the space devoted to their description and modes of cultivation in the Horticultural Press.

In the hope, too, of helping to establish a much-desired standard of nomenclature, I have followed the generic names adopted by the authors of "The Genera Plantarum," and the specific names and orthography, as far as I have been able, of the "Index Kewensis"; and where possible I have given the synonyms, the date of introduction, and the native country. The alphabetical arrangement that has been adopted, both with regard to the genera and species, it is hoped, will greatly facilitate the work of reference to its pages. The descriptive notes and hints on cultivation, the selected lists of Trees and Shrubs for various special purposes, and the calendarial list which indicates the flowering season of the different species, may be considered all the more valuable for being concisely written, and made readily accessible by means of the Index.

No work written on a similar plan and treating solely of Hardy Ornamental Flowering Trees and Shrubs has hitherto been published; and it is not supposed for a moment that the present one will entirely supply the deficiency; but should it meet with any measure of public approval, it may be the means of paving the way towards the publication of a more elaborate work—and one altogether more worthy of the interesting and beautiful Flowering Trees and Shrubs that have been found suitable for planting in the climate of the British Isles.

Of the fully thirteen hundred species and varieties of Trees and Shrubs enumerated, all may be depended upon as being hardy in some part of the country. Several of them, and particularly those introduced from China and Japan, have not before been included in a book of this character. Trials for the special purpose of testing the hardiness of the more tender kinds have been instituted and carried out in several favoured parts of England and Ireland.

A. D. W.

CONTENTS

HARDY ORNAMENTAL FLOWERING TREES AND SHRUBS

Abelia (Caprifoliaceæ).

ABELIA CHINENSIS (*syn A. rupestris*).—The Rock Abelia, China, 1844. This is a neat, twiggy shrub, growing from 2 feet to 3 feet high, with slender shoots, and very pleasing, shining green serrated leaves. The tubular, sweet-scented flowers are produced in clusters at the ends of the shoots, even the smallest, and are of a very delicate shade of pink—indeed, almost white. It makes an excellent wall plant, but by no means refuses to grow and flower freely without either shelter or protection, if a fairly rich and well-drained soil is provided. From August to October is the flowering period of this handsome deciduous shrub. It is the only really hardy species of the genus, for though the rosy-purple-flowered A. floribunda (Mexico, 1842) and A. serrata (China, 1844) have stood for several years uninjured in the South of England, they are not to be relied upon. All the species are readily propagated from cuttings.

A. TRIFLORA.—Himalayan regions, 1847. A half-hardy and beautiful species with small lanceolate, entire leaves, and pretty star-shaped flowers that are yellowish-white and flushed with pink. The long, narrow, and hairy calyx-lobes give a light and feathery appearance to the flowers, which are produced continuously from May to November. It does best as a wall plant, and several beautiful examples may be seen in and around London, as also at Exeter, and in the South of Ireland.

Acacia. See Robinia.

Acanthopanax. See Aralia.

Acer (Sapindaceæ).

Though less remarkable for beauty of flowers than for their neatly-divided and often brightly-tinted foliage, yet a few species of Acer must be ranked as amongst the most ornamental and attractive of early-flowering trees. Such would include A. RUBRUM (the Scarlet Maple, Canada, 1656), with vivid scarlet flowers; A. STRIATUM (North America, 1755), which has large and conspicuous flowers on long peduncles and curious black-and-white longitudinal markings on the smooth, bright-green bark; A. TARTARICUM (1759), in which the crowded racemes of yellowish-green flowers are tinged with red; and our commonest of all A. PLATANOIDES (the Norway Maple, Europe, 1683), which is one of the showiest in early spring. They succeed well in loam or alluvial deposit.

Actinidia (Ternstroemiaceæ).

ACTINIDIA CHINENSIS.—China, 1847. Whether for its curious and ornamental foliage or clusters of showy yellow flowers this little-known Chinese climbing plant is well worthy of extended cultivation in this country. It is quite hardy, and when established in suitable soil grows away freely. The long-stalked, sub-orbicular leaves, which measure 3 inches to 4 inches across, are rendered particularly noticeable on account of the dense covering of deep-red hairs with which, especially in a young state, both these and the shoots are covered. The clustered yellow flowers are borne on short spurs, and are about 1½ inch in diameter. It succeeds well around London, and seems to prefer a northern aspect.

A. KOLOMIKTA.—North-East Asia, 1880. This is a rare species with serrated leaves and small white flowers.

A. POLYGAMA (Japan, 1870) and A. VOLUBILIS (Japan, 1874) both produce white flowers, the former having heart-shaped and the latter oval leaves. They are rare in cultivation and require a warm, rich soil and sheltered site.

Adenocarpus (Leguminosæ).

ADENOCARPUS DECORTICANS (*syn A. Boissieri*).—Spain, 1883. This little-known, hardy shrub, a native of the Sierra Nevada mountains, in Spain, is one of great beauty, and well worthy of extended culture. The flowers are produced abundantly, and are of a bright yellow colour, resembling those of our common Broom, to which family it is nearly allied. Peaty soil suits it well, and repeated trials have clearly proved that it is hardy, at least in the South of England.

Ægle. See Citrus.

Æsculus (Sapindaceæ).

ÆSCULUS CALIFORNICA (*syn Pavia californica*).—California. This is one of the handsomest species, of low, spreading habit, with white or pale-rose fragrant flowers produced freely about midsummer. It rarely exceeds 15 feet in height.

Æ. CARNEA (*syn Æ. rubicunda*).—Red-flowered Horse Chestnut. North America, 1820. If only for its neat and moderate growth, and attractive spikes of brightly-coloured flowers, this species must be considered as one of the handsomest and most valuable of small growing trees. Being of moderate size—for we rarely meet with specimens of greater height than 30 feet—and of very compact habit, it is rendered peculiarly suitable for planting in confined spots, and where larger growing and more spreading subjects would be out of place. It withstands soot and smoke well, and is therefore much valued for suburban planting. The long spikes of pretty scarlet flowers are usually produced in great abundance, and as they stand well above the foliage, and are of firm lasting substance, they have a most pleasing and attractive appearance. As there are numerous forms of the red-flowered Horse Chestnut, differing much in the depth of flower colouring, it may be well to warn planters, for some of these have but a faint tinge of pink overlaying a dirty yellowish-green groundwork, while the finest and most desirable tree has the flowers of a decided pinky-red. There is a double-flowered variety Æ. carnea flore-pleno (*syn Æ. rubicunda flore-pleno*), and one of particular merit named Æ. rubicunda Briotii.

Æ. HIPPOCASTANUM.—The Common Horse Chestnut. Asia, 1629. A fine, hardy, free-flowering tree, supposed to have been introduced from Asia, and of which there are several varieties, including a double-flowered, a variegated, and several lobed and cut-leaved forms. The tree needs no description, the spikes of pinky-white flowers, which are produced in great abundance, and ample foliage rendering it one of, if not the handsomest tree of our acquaintance. It gives a pleasing shade, and forms an imposing and picturesque object in the landscape, especially where the conditions of soil—a rich free loam—are provided. Æ. Hippocastanum alba flore-pleno (the double white Horse Chestnut) has a decidedly pyramidal habit of growth, and the flowers, which are larger than those of the species, are perfectly double. It is a very distinct and desirable large-growing tree. Æ. Hippocastanum laciniata and Æ. Hippocastanum digitalis are valuable for their divided leaves; while Æ. Hippocastanum foliis variegatis has the foliage rather irregularly variegated.

Æ. PARVIFLORA (*syn Pavia macrostachya*).—Buckeye. North America, 1820. This is very distinct, and possesses features which are shared by no other hardy tree or shrub in cultivation. Rarely exceeding 12 feet in height, and with a spread of often as much as 20 feet, this shrub forms a perfect hemisphere of foliage, which, when tipped with the pretty fragrant flowers, renders it one of the most effective and handsome. The foliage is large, and resembles that of the common Horse Chestnut, while the pure white flowers, with their long, projecting stamens and red-tipped anthers, are very pretty and imposing when at their best in July. It succeeds well in rich, dampish loam, and as a shrub for standing alone in any conspicuous position it has, indeed, few equals.

Æ. Pavia (*syn Pavia rubra*).—Red Buckeye. North America, 1711. A small-growing and slender-branched tree or shrub, which bears an abundance of brownish-scarlet flowers. There are several good varieties, two of the best being Æ. Pavia atrosanguinea, and Æ. Pavia Whittleyana, with small, brilliant red flowers.

Æ. turbinate.—Japan, 1888. In general appearance this desirable new species closely resembles our common Horse Chestnut. The flowers are white, succeeded by smooth fruit about the size of those of the commonly cultivated tree. It is quite hardy, and thrives well in light loamy soil.

There are several other species, such as Æ. Pavia humilis (*syn Pavia humilis*), of trailing habit; Æ. flava (*syn Pavia flava*), bearing pretty yellow flowers; Æ. Pavia macrocarpa (*syn Pavia macrocarpa*), an open-headed and graceful tree; Æ. flava discolor (*syn Pavia discolor*); and Æ. glabra, the "Ohio Buck-eye"; but they have not been found very amenable to cultivation, except in very favoured parts of the South of England and Ireland.

Ailanthus (Xanthoxylaceæ). See Cedrela.

Ailanthus glandulosa.—Tree of Heaven. China, 1751. A handsome, fast-growing tree, with large pinnate leaves that are often fully 3 feet long, and terminal erect clusters of not very showy greenish-white flowers that exhale a rather disagreeable odour. It is one of the most distinct and imposing of pinnate-leaved trees, and forms a neat specimen for the lawn or park, while the autumn colour of foliage is particularly rich. Light loam on a gravelly subsoil suits it well.

Akebia (Lardizabalaceæ).

Akebia quinata.—Chinese Akebia. China, 1845. This, with its peculiarly-formed and curiously-coloured flowers, though usually treated as a cool greenhouse plant, is yet sufficiently hardy to grow and flower well in many of the southern and western English counties, where it has stood uninjured for many years. It is a pretty twining evergreen, with the leaves placed on long slender petioles, and palmately divided into usually five leaflets. The sweet-scented flowers, particularly so in the evening, are of a purplish-brown or scarlet-purple, and produced in axillary racemes of from ten to a dozen in each. For covering trellis-work, using as a wall plant, or to clamber over some loose-growing specimen shrub, from which a slight protection will also be afforded, the Akebia is peculiarly suitable, and soon ascends to a height of 10 feet or 12 feet. Any ordinary garden soil suits it, and propagation by cutting is readily effected.

Aloysia. See Lippia.

Althæa. See Hibiscus.

Amelanchier (Rosaceæ).

Amelanchier alnifolia.—Dwarf June Berry. North-West America, 1888. This is a shrub of great beauty, growing about 8 feet high, and a native of the mountains from British America to California. It differs from A. canadensis in having much larger and more brilliant-tinted fruit, and in its shorter and more compact racemes of white flower. The shape of the leaves cannot be depended on as a point of recognition, those before me, collected in the native habitat of the plant, differing to a wide extent in size and shape, some being coarsely serrated while others are almost entire. Light soil suits it well.

A. CANADENSIS.—June Berry. Canada, 1746. Unquestionably this is one of the most beautiful and showy of early flowering trees. During the month of April the profusion of snow-white flowers, with which even young specimens are mantled, render the plant conspicuous for a long way off, while in autumn the golden yellow of the dying-off foliage is quite as remarkable. Being perfectly hardy, of free growth, and with no particular desire for certain classes of soils, the June Berry should be widely planted for ornamental effect. In this country it attains to a height of 40 feet, and bears globose crimson fruit. There are several varieties, including A. canadensis rotundifolia, A. canadensis oblongifolia, and A. canadensis oligocarpa, the latter being by some botanists ranked as a species.

A. VULGARIS.—Common Amelanchier. South of Europe, 1596. This is the only European species, and grows about 16 feet in height. It has been in cultivation in this country for over 300 years. Generally this species flowers earlier than the American ones, has rounder and less deeply serrated leaves, but the flowers are much alike. A. vulgaris cretica, from Crete and Dalmatia, is readily distinguished by the soft white hairs with which the undersides of the leaves are thickly covered. To cultivate the Amelanchiers successfully a good rich but light soil is a necessity, while shelter from cutting winds must be afforded if the sheets of flowers are to be seen in their best form.

Amorpha (Leguminosæ).

Amorpha canescens.—Lead Plant. Missouri, 1812. This is of much smaller growth than A. fruticosa, with neat pinnate foliage, whitened with hoary down, and bearing panicles of bluish-purple flowers, with conspicuous orange anthers. It is a charming shrub, and all the more valuable as it flowers at the end of summer, when few hardy plants are in bloom. To grow it satisfactorily a dry, sandy soil is a necessity.

A. fruticosa.—False Indigo. Carolina, 1724. This is a fast-growing shrub fully 6 feet high, of loose, upright habit, and with pretty pinnate leaves. The flowers are borne in densely packed spikes, are of a purplish tint with bright-yellow protruding anthers, and produced at the end of summer. It prefers a dry, warm soil of a sandy or chalky nature, and may readily be increased from cuttings or suckers, the latter being freely produced. Hard cutting back when full size has been attained would seem to throw fresh vigour into the Amorpha, and the flowering is greatly enhanced by such a mode of treatment. A native of Carolina, and perfectly hardy in most parts of the country. Of this species there are several varieties, amongst others, A. fruticosa nana, a dwarf, twiggy plant; A. fruticosa dealbata, with lighter green foliage than the type; and others differing only in the size and width of the leaves.

Amygdalus. See Prunus.

Andromeda (Ericaceæ). See Cassandra, Cassiope, Leucothoe, Lyonia, Oxydendrum, Pieris, and Zenobia.

Andromeda polifolia.—An indigenous shrub of low growth, with lanceolate shining leaves, and pretty globose pinky-white flowers. Of it there are two varieties, A. polifolia major and A. polifolia angustifolia, both well worthy of culture for their neat habit and pretty flowers. Light peaty soil suits its wants.

Aralia (Araliaceæ). See Fatsia.

ARALIA MANDSHURICA (*syn Dimorphanthus mandschuricus*).—Manchuria, 1866. There is not much beauty about this Chinese tree, for here it is but a big spiny stake, 10 feet to 12 feet high, with no branches, and a tuft of palm-like foliage at the top. The flowers, however, are both large and conspicuous, and impart to the tree an interesting and novel appearance about midsummer. They are individually small, of a creamy-white colour, and produced in long, umbellate racemes, which when fully developed, from their weight and terminal position, are tilted gracefully to one side. Usually the stem is spiny, with Horse Chestnut-like bark, while the terminal bud, from its large size, as if all the energy of the plant was concentrated in the tip, imparts a curious and somewhat ungainly appearance to the tree. From its curious tropical appearance this species is well worthy of a place in the shrubbery. It is unmindful of soil, if that is of at all fair quality, and may be said to be perfectly hardy over the greater part of the country.

A. MANDSHURICA ALBO-MARGINATUS is a desirable variety with an irregular silvery edging to the leaves.

A. MAXIMOWICZII (*Acanthopanax ricinifolium*).—Japan, 1874. A noble tree of elegant appearance, with spiral stems, and large lobed leaves almost similar to those of the castor-oil plant. The flowers are greenish-white, and the tree succeeds best in dampish loam.

A. SPINOSA.—Angelica Tree. Virginia, 1688. Amongst autumn-flowering shrubs this takes a high place, for in mild seasons it blooms well into October. It grows about

12 feet high, with large tri-pinnate leaves, composed of numerous serrulate leaflets. The individual flowers are small and whitish, but being borne in large-branched panicles have a very imposing appearance. It is of free growth, and produces suckers abundantly.

Arbutus (Ericaceæ). See Pernettya.

ARBUTUS ANDRACHNE.—Levant, 1724. This Mediterranean species is of stout growth, with narrow Laurel-like leaves, reddish deciduous bark, and greenish-white flowers that are produced freely in May. A hybrid form, said to have originated between this species and A. Unedo, partakes in part of the nature of both shrubs, but the flowers are larger than those of A. Unedo. Both thrive well in light loamy soil.

A MENZIESII (*syn A. procera.*)—Tall Strawberry Tree. North-West America, 1827. This is hardy in many parts of these islands, particularly maritime districts, and is worthy of culture if only for the large racemose panicles of deliciously-scented white flowers, and peculiar metallic-green leaves. The fruit is orange-red, and only about half the size of that of our commonly cultivated species.

A. UNEDO.—Strawberry Tree. Ireland. This is a beautiful evergreen shrub or small-growing tree, sometimes fully 20 feet high, with ovate-lanceolate leaves, and clusters of pure white or yellowish-tinged flowers appearing in September and October. The bright scarlet fruit, about the size of and resembling a strawberry, is highly ornamental, and when borne in quantity imparts to the plant an unusual and very attractive appearance. Generally speaking, the Arbutus is hardy, although in inland situations it is sometimes killed to the ground in severe winters, but, springing freely from the root, the plant soon becomes re-established. In a young state it suffers too, but after becoming established and a few feet high, the chances of injury are greatly minimized. Three well-marked varieties are A. Unedo coccinea and A. Unedo rubra, bearing scarlet and deep-red flowers, and A. Unedo microphylla, with much smaller leaves than those of the parent plant.

A. Unedo Croomei differs considerably from the former, in having larger foliage, larger clusters of reddish-pink flowers, and the bark of the young shoots of an enticing ruddy, or rather brownish-red colour. It is a very desirable and highly ornamental plant, and one that is well worthy of extended culture.

There are several others, to wit A. photiniæfolia, A. Rollissoni, A. Millerii, with large leaves, and pretty pink flowers, and A. serratifolia, having deeply serrated leaves. Deep, light loam, if on chalk all the better, and a fairly warm and sheltered situation, would seem to suit the Arbutus best.

Arctostaphylos (Ericaceæ).

Arctostaphylos alpina.—Black Bearberry. Scotland. This is confined to the Northern Highlands of Scotland, is of neat habit of growth, with toothed, deciduous leaves, and small drooping white flowers, two or three together. Both this and the following are suitable for the rock garden, where they thrive in light, peaty soil.

A. Uva-ursi.—Bearberry. Britain. A neat shrub of trailing habit, and with pinkish flowers resembling those of the Arbutus, but much smaller. The leaves are entire, dark green in colour, about an inch long, and obovate or oblong in shape. Fruit globular, of a bright red, smooth and shining. This is a native shrub, being found in Scotland, Northern England, and Ireland.

Aristolochia (Aristolochiaceæ).

Aristolochia Sipho.—Dutchman's Pipe. North America, 1763. A large-growing, deciduous, climbing shrub, remarkable for its ample foliage, and curiously formed yellow and purple streaked flowers. A native of North America, it is perfectly hardy in this country, and makes an excellent wall plant where plenty of space can be afforded for the rambling branches. What a pity it is that so ornamental a climber, whose big, dark-green leaves overlap each other as if intended for keeping a house cool in warm weather, is not more generally planted! It does well and grows fast in almost any soil.

Aristotelia (Tiliaceæ).

Aristotelia Macqui.—Chili, 1733. A half-hardy shrub, with oblong, toothed leaves and inconspicuous greenish flowers which are succeeded by purple berries. A warm situation is necessary, and light, rich soil.

Artemisia (Compositæ).

Artemisia Abrotanum.—Southerwood, Europe, 1548. A small-growing shrub with highly aromatic, deep-green, rue-like foliage, and a plentiful supply of small, dirty-yellow flowers. It is interesting, but of no great value in an ornamental sense.

Asimina (Anonaceæ).

Asimina triloba.—Virginian Papaw. Pennsylvania, 1736. This is a curious and uncommon shrub that one rarely sees outside the walls of a botanic garden. The flowers are dark purple or chocolate brown, fully 2 inches across, and succeeded by a yellow, oblong, pulpy fruit, that is relished by the natives, and from which the name of North American Custard Apple has been derived. In this country it is quite at home, growing around London to quite 12 feet in height, but it wants a warm, dry soil and sunny sheltered situation. As a wall plant it does best.

Aster. See Microglossa.

Atragene. See Clematis.

Atriplex (Chenopodiaceæ).

Atriplex halimus.—Mediterranean Region, 1640. This is a sea-coast shrub of dwarf habit, the ovate, oblong leaves being thickly clothed with a greyish, scaly indumentum.

It is quite hardy, and being of dwarf, spreading growth is to be recommended, although the flowers are by no means attractive.

Azalea. See Rhododendron.

Azara (Bixineæ).

Azara microphylla.—Chili, 1873. This is the only recognized hardy species, and probably the best from an ornamental point of view. In mild seaside districts it may succeed as a standard in the open ground, but generally it is cultivated as a wall plant, for which it is peculiarly suitable. The small, dark-green, glossy leaves are thickly arranged on the nearly horizontal branches, while the greenish flowers, if they lack in point of showiness, are deliciously fragrant and plentifully produced. For wall-covering, especially in an eastern aspect, it is one of the neatest of shrubs.

Other species in cultivation are A. serrata, A. lanceolata, and A. integrifolia, but for general planting, and unless under the most favoured conditions, they are not to be recommended. The Azaras are by no means particular about the quality of soil in which they are planted, and succeed well even in stiffish loam, bordering on clay.

Baccharis (Compositæ).

BACCHARIS HALIMIFOLIA.—Groundsel Tree or Sea Purslane. North America, 1683. For seaside planting this is an invaluable shrub, as it succeeds well down even to high-water mark, and where it is almost lashed by the salt spray. The flowers are not very ornamental, resembling somewhat those of the Groundsel, but white with a tint of purple. Leaves obovate in shape, notched, and thickly covered with a whitish powder, which imparts to them a pleasing glaucous hue. Any light soil that is tolerably dry suits well the wants of this shrub, but it is always seen in best condition by the seaside. Under favourable conditions it attains to a height of 12 feet, with a branch spread nearly as much in diameter. A native of the North American coast from Maryland to Florida.

B. PATAGONICA.—Megallan. This is a very distinct and quite hardy species, with small, deep-green leaves and white flowers. It succeeds under the same conditions as the latter.

Baptisia. See Piptanthus.

Benthamia. See Cornus.

Berberidopsis (Berberidaceæ).

BERBERIDOPSIS CORALLINA. — Coral Barberry. Chili, 1862. This handsome evergreen, half-climbing shrub is certainly not so well known as its merits entitle it to be. Unfortunately it is not hardy in every part of the country, though in the southern and western English counties, but especially within the influence of the sea, it succeeds well as a wall plant, and charms us with its globular, waxy, crimson or coral-red flowers. The spiny-toothed leaves approach very near those of some of the Berberis, with which the plant is nearly allied. It seems to do best in a partially shady situation, and in rich, light loam.

Berberis (Berberidaceæ).

BERBERIS AQUIFOLIUM (*syn Mahonia aquifolium*).—Holly-leaved Barberry. North America, 1823. This justly ranks as one of the handsomest, most useful, and easily-cultivated of all hardy shrubs. It will grow almost anywhere, and in any class of soil, though preferring a fairly rich loam. Growing under favourable conditions to a height of 6 feet, this North American shrub forms a dense mass of almost impenetrable foliage. The leaves are large, dark shining green, and thickly beset with spines, while the deliciously-scented yellow flowers, which are produced at each branch tip, render the plant particularly attractive in spring. It is still further valuable both on account of the rich autumnal tint of the foliage, and pretty plum colour of the plentifully produced fruit.

B. AQUIFOLIUM REPENS (*syn Mahonia repens*).—Creeping Barberry. North America, 1822. This is of altogether smaller growth than the preceding, but otherwise they seem nearly allied. From its dense, dwarf growth, rising as it rarely does more than a foot from the ground, and neat foliage, this Barberry is particularly suitable for edging beds, or forming a low evergreen covering for rocky ground or mounds.

B. ARGUTA (*syn Mahonia arguta*).—This undescribed species was sent to Kew from the Botanic Gardens at Dublin in 1907. The leathery leaves have five pairs of leaflets, and the lemon-yellow flowers are in erect crowded panicles. It is closely allied to Mahonia paniculata.

B. ARISTATA, a native of Nepaul (1820), is a vigorous-growing species, resembling somewhat our native plant, with deeply serrated leaves, brightly tinted bark, and yellow flowers. It is of erect spreading habit, and in winter is rendered very conspicuous by reason of the bright-reddish colour of the leafless branches.

B. Bealei (*syn Mahonia Beallii*).—Japan, 1887. This species is one of the first to appear in bloom, often by the end of January the plant being thickly studded with flowers. It is a handsome shrub, of erect habit, the leaves of a yellowish-green tint, and furnished with long, spiny teeth. The clusters of racemes of deliciously fragrant yellow flowers are of particular value, as being produced so early in the season. This is sometimes included under B. japonica.

B. buxifolia (*syn B. dulcis* and *B. microphylla*).—Straits of Magellan, 1830. A neat and erect-growing shrub of somewhat stiff and upright habit, and bearing tiny yellow flowers. This is a good rockwork plant, and being of neat habit, with small purplish leaves, is well worthy of cultivation.

B. congestiflora.—Chili, 1861, is not yet well known, but promises to become a general favourite with lovers of hardy shrubs. It is of unusual appearance for a Barberry, with long, decumbent branches, which are thickly covered with masses of orange-yellow flowers. The branch-tips, being almost leafless and smothered with flowers, impart to the plant a striking but distinctly ornamental appearance.

B. Darwinii.—Chili, 1849. This is, perhaps, the best known and most ornamental of the family. It forms a dense bush, sometimes 10 feet high, with dark, glossy leaves, and dense racemes of orange-yellow flowers, produced in April and May, and often again in the autumn.

B. empetrifolia.—Straits of Magellan, 1827. This is a neat-habited and dwarf evergreen shrub, that even under the best cultivation rarely exceeds 2 feet in height. It is one of the hardiest species, and bears, though rather sparsely, terminal golden-yellow flowers, which are frequently produced both in spring and autumn. For its compact growth and neat foliage it is alone worthy of culture.

B. Fortunei (*syn Mahonia Fortunei*).—China, 1846.

This is rather a rare species in cultivation, with finely-toothed leaves, composed of about seven leaflets, and bearing in abundance clustered racemes of individually small yellow flowers. A native of China, and requiring a warm, sunny spot to do it justice.

B. GRACILIS (*syn Mahonia gracilis*).—Mexico. A pretty, half-hardy species, growing about 6 feet high, with slender branches, and shining green leaves with bright-red stalks. Flowers small, in 3-inch long racemes, deep yellow with bright-red pedicels. Fruit globular, deep purple.

B. ILICIFOLIA (*syn B. Neumanii*).—South America, 1791. This is another handsome evergreen species from South America, and requires protection in this country. The thick, glossy-green leaves, beset with spines, and large orange-red flowers, combine to make this shrub one of great interest and beauty.

B. JAPONICA (*syn Mahonia japonica*).—China and Japan. This is not a very satisfactory shrub in these isles, although in warm seaside districts, and when planted in rich loam, on a gravelly subsoil, it forms a handsome plant with noble foliage, and deliciously fragrant yellow flowers. B. Beali and B. intermedia are supposed forms.

B. NEPALENSIS (*syn Mahonia nepalensis*).—Nepaul Barberry. This is a noble Himalayan species that one rarely sees in good condition in this country, unless when protected by glass. The long, chalky-white stems, often rising to 8 feet in height, are surmounted by dense clusters of lemon-yellow flowers. Planted outdoors, this handsome and partly evergreen Barberry must have the protection of a wall.

B. NERVOSA (*syn Mahonia glumacea*).—North America, 1826. This, with its terminal clusters of reddish-yellow flowers produced in spring, is a highly attractive North-West American species. It is of neat and compact growth, perfectly hardy, but as yet it is rare in cultivation. The autumnal leafage tint is very attractive.

B. PINNATA (*syn Mahonia fascicularis*).—A native of

Mexico (1820), this species is of stout growth, with long leaves, that are thickly furnished with sharp spines. The yellow flowers are produced abundantly, and being in large bunches render the plant very conspicuous. It is, unfortunately, not very hardy, and requires wall protection to do it justice.

B. SINENSIS.—China, 1815. This is a really handsome and distinct species, with twiggy, deciduous branches, from the undersides of the arching shoots of which the flowers hang in great profusion. They are greenish-yellow inside, but of a dark brownish-crimson without, while the leaves are small and round, and die off crimson in autumn.

B. STENOPHYLLA, a hybrid between B. Darwinii and B. empetrifolia, is one of the handsomest forms in cultivation, the wealth of golden-yellow flowers being remarkable, as is also the dark purple berries. It is very hardy, and of the freest growth.

B. TRIFOLIATA (*syn Mahonia trifoliata*).—Mexico, 1839. This is a very distinct and beautiful Mexican species that will only succeed around London as a wall plant. It grows about a yard high, with leaves fully 3 inches long, having three terminal sessile leaflets, and slender leaf stalks often 2 inches long. The ternate leaflets are of a glaucous blue colour, marbled with dull green, and very delicately veined. Flowers small, bright yellow, and produced in few-flowered axillary racemes on short peduncles. The berries are small, globular, and light red.

B. TRIFURCA (*syn Mahonia trifurca*).—China, 1852. This is an evergreen shrub of neat, low growth, with three-forked leaflets, but it does not appear to be at all plentiful.

B. VULGARIS.—Common Barberry. This is a native species, with oblong leaves, and terminal, drooping racemes of yellow flowers. It is chiefly valued for the great wealth of orange-scarlet fruit. There are two very distinct forms, one bearing silvery and the other black fruit, and named respectively B. vulgaris fructo-albo and B. vulgaris fructo-nigro.

B. Wallichiana (*syn B. Hookeri*).—Nepaul, 1820. This is exceedingly ornamental, whether as regards the foliage, flowers, or fruit. It is of dense, bushy growth, with large, dark-green spiny leaves, and an abundance of clusters of clear yellow flowers. The berries are deep violet-purple, and fully half an inch long. Being perfectly hardy and of free growth it is well suited for extensive planting.

B. Wilsonæ.—China. This recently-introduced Barberry is of dwarf growth, rarely exceeding 3 feet in height, with small, spatulate leaves arranged in fascicles along the stem, and yellow flowers which are rendered conspicuous by reason of the bright-red stamens. The flowers, which appear in spring, are succeeded by a wealth of globular red berries, while the beautifully tinted foliage renders the plant one of particular interest during October. Being of drooping habit, with gracefully arching branches, the shrub is rendered peculiarly suitable for the higher ledges in rock gardening. It does not seem particular as to soil, thriving well in peaty loam. Collected in Central China by Mr. E. H. Wilson.

Berchemia (Rhamnaceæ).

Berchemia racemosa (Japan, 1888) has small flowers in terminal panicles which are succeeded by brown berries.

B. volubilis.—Climbing Berchemia. Carolina, 1714. A rarely seen, deciduous climber, bearing rather inconspicuous greenish-white flowers, succeeded by attractive, violet-tinted berries. The foliage is neat and pretty, the individual leaves being ovate in shape and slightly undulated or wavy. It is a twining shrub that in this country, even under favourable circumstances, one rarely sees ascending to a greater height than about 12 feet. Sandy peat and a shady site suits it best, and so placed it will soon cover a low-growing tree or bush much in the way that our common Honeysuckle does. It is propagated from layers or cuttings.

Bignonia (Bignoniaceæ). See Tecoma.

BIGNONIA CAPREOLATA.—Virginia and other parts of America, 1710. This is not so hardy as to be depended upon throughout the country generally, though in the milder parts of England and Ireland it succeeds well as a wall plant. It is a handsome climbing shrub, with long, heart-shaped leaves, usually terminating in branched tendrils, and large, orange flowers produced singly from April to August.

Billardiera (Pittosporeaceæ).

BILLARDIERA LONGIFLORA.—Blue Apple Berry. Van Diemen's Land, 1810. If only for its rich, blue berries, as large as those of a cherry, this otherwise elegant climbing shrub is well worthy of a far greater share of attention than it has yet received, for it must be admitted that it is far from common. The greenish bell-shaped blossoms produced in May are, perhaps, not very attractive, but this is more than compensated for by the highly ornamental fruit, which renders the plant an object of great beauty about mid-September. Leaves small and narrow, on slender, twining stems, that clothe well the lower half of a garden wall in some sunny favoured spot. Cuttings root freely if inserted in sharp sand and placed in slight heat, while seeds germinate quickly.

Bridgesia. See Ercilla.

Bryanthus (Ericaceæ).

BRYANTHUS BREWERI (1896) is a desirable small-growing evergreen, with short, crowded, almost smooth leaves, and short racemes of large rosy-purple flowers.

B. EMPETRIFORMIS (*syn Menziesia empetrifolia*).—North-West America, 1829. This is a compact, neat species, and well suited for alpine gardening. The flowers are rosy-purple, and produced abundantly.

B. ERECTUS.—Siberia. This is a pretty little Ericaceous plant, nearly allied to Menziesia, and supposed to be of hybrid origin. The flowers, which are borne in crowded clusters at the points of the shoots, are bell-shaped, and of a pleasing reddish-lilac colour. It wants a cool, moist, peaty soil, and is perfectly hardy. When in a flowering stage this Bryanthus is one of the brightest occupants of the peat bed, and is a very suitable companion for such dwarf plants as the Heaths, Menziesias, and smaller growing Kalmias.

B. GMELINI.—Kamtschatka and Behrings Island. This is of dwarf growth, and bears an abundance of red flowers.

Buddleia (Loganiaceæ).

BUDDLEIA COLVILEI.—Himalaya, Sikkim. Though not generally hardy in Britain, yet in the warmer parts it blossoms freely. The flowers are bell-shaped and of a deep rose colour, shaded with red, and freely produced at the branch tips. It does well in a gravelly soil and where fully exposed to the sunshine.

B. GLOBOSA. — Orange Ball Tree. Chili, 1774. A shrubby species, ranging in height from 12 feet to 20 feet, and the only one at all common in gardens. Favoured spots in Southern England would seem to suit this plant fairly well, but to see it at its best one must visit some of the maritime gardens of North Wales, where it grows stout and strong, and flowers with amazing luxuriance. Where it thrives it must be ranked amongst the most beautiful of wall plants, for few, indeed, are the standard specimens that are to be met with, the protection afforded by a wall being almost a necessity in its cultivation. The leaves are linear-lanceolate, and covered with a dense silvery tomentum on the undersides, somewhat rugose above, and partially deciduous. Flowers in small globular heads, bright orange or yellow, and being plentifully produced are very showy in early summer. It succeeds well in rich moist loam on gravel.

B. LINDLEYANA.—China, 1844. This has purplish-red flowers and angular twigs, but its hardihood cannot be relied upon unless in very sheltered and mild parts of the country.

B. PANICULATA (*syn B. crispa*).—Nepaul, 1823. This may at once be distinguished by its curly, woolly leaves, and fragrant lilac flowers. It is a desirable species, but suffers from our climate.

B. VARIABILIS.—China, 1896. A desirable, tall-growing species that is remarkable both for its whitish, woolly appearance and abundantly produced lavender or rosy-purple flowers. The foliage varies much in size and shape, and the shrub does well when planted in smoky localities. The variety Veitchiana is one of the best.

Two other rare species are B. ALBIFLORA (China), with mauve and orange flowers, and B. ASIATICA (India, 1874), of small growth with white sweet-scented flowers; while B. japonica has dense spikes of pale-lilac flowers.

Bupleurum (Umbelliferæ).

BUPLEURUM FRUTICOSUM.—Hare's Ear. South Europe, 1596. A small-growing, branching shrub, with obovate-lanceolate leaves, and compound umbels of yellowish flowers. It is more curious than beautiful.

Cæsalpinia (Leguminosæ).

CÆSALPINIA SEPIARIA (*syn C. japonica*).—Japan, 1888. This is as yet a comparatively little known shrub, but one that from its beauty and hardihood is sure to become a general favourite. Planted out in a light, sandy, peaty soil, and where fully exposed, this shrub has done well, and proved itself a suitable subject for the climate of England at least. The hard prickles with which both stem and branches are provided render the shrub of rather formidable appearance, while the leaves are of a peculiarly pleasing soft-green tint. For the flowers, too, it is well worthy of attention, the pinky anthers contrasting so markedly with the deep yellow of the other portions of the flower. They are arranged in long racemes, and show well above the foliage.

Calluna (Ericaceæ). See Erica.

CALLUNA VULGARIS (*syn Erica vulgaris*).—Common Ling or Heather. This is the commonest native species, with purplish-pink flowers on small pedicels. There are many very distinct and beautiful-flowering forms, the following being some of the best: C. vulgaris alba, white-flowered; C. vulgaris Hammondi, C. vulgaris minor, and C. vulgaris pilosa, all white-flowered forms; C. vulgaris Alportii, and C. vulgaris Alportii variegata, the former bearing rich crimson flowers, and the latter with distinctly variegated foliage; C. vulgaris argentea, and C. vulgaris aurea, with silvery-variegated and golden foliage; C. vulgaris flore-pleno, a most beautiful and free-growing variety, with double flowers; C. vulgaris Foxii, a dwarf plant that does not flower freely; and C. vulgaris pumila, and C. vulgaris dumosa, which are of small cushion-like growth. They succeed best in peaty loam.

Calophaca (Leguminosæ).

CALOPHACA WOLGARICA.—Siberia, 1786. This member of the Pea family is of dwarf, branching growth, thickly clothed with glandular hairs, and bears yellow flowers, which are succeeded by reddish-purple pods. It is of no special importance as an ornamental shrub, and is most frequently seen grafted on the Laburnum, though its natural easy habit of growth is far preferable. Hailing from Siberia, it may be considered as fairly hardy at least.

Calycanthus (Calycanthaceæ).

Calycanthus floridus.—Carolina Allspice. Carolina, 1726. If only for the purplish-red, pleasantly-scented flowers, this North American shrub is worthy of extensive culture. The hardiness, accommodating nature and delicious perfume of its brightly-coloured flowers render this shrub one of the choicest subjects for the shrubbery or margin of the woodland path. It is of easy though compact growth, reaching in favourable situations a height of 12 feet, and with ovate leaves that are slightly pubescent. Growing best in good, fairly moist loam, where partial shade is afforded, the sides of woodland drives and paths will suit this Allspice well; but it wants plenty of room for branch-development. There are several nursery forms of this shrub, such as C. floridus glaucus, C. floridus asplenifolia, and C. floridus nanus, all probably distinct enough, but of no superior ornamental value to the parent plant.

C. occidentalis.—Californian or Western Allspice. California, 1831. This is larger in all its parts than the former, and for decorative purposes is even preferable to that species. The flowers are dark crimson or purple, and nearly twice as large as those of C. floridus, but rather more sparsely produced. It is a very distinct and desirable shrub, and one that can be recommended for lawn and park planting, but, like the former, it delights to grow in a rather moist and shady situation.

C. præcox.—See Chimonanthus fragrans.

Camellia (Ternstræmiaceæ).

Camellia japonica.—Japan and China, 1739. In the warmer parts of England this species flourishes out of doors, but a sheltered, sunny site must be chosen. The flowers are deep-red in colour and well set off by the shining green leaves, which are sharply dentated. There are many hybrids of this species. It does best when planted in a mixture of loam and peat.

C. SASANQUA.—Japan. A fragile shrub that wants the protection of a wall. There are two varieties, one bearing double white and the other single red flowers in the richest abundance.

Caprifolium. See Lonicera.

Caragana (Leguminosæ).

CARAGANA ALTAGANA.—Dahuria, 1789. A shrub about a yard high, with six to eight pairs of glabrous, obovate leaves and yellow flowers, produced from April to July.

C. ARBORESCENS.—Siberian Pea Tree. Siberia, 1752. On account of its great hardiness, this is a very desirable garden shrub or small-growing tree. The bright-yellow, pea-shaped flowers are very attractive, while the deep-green, pinnate foliage imparts to the tree a somewhat unusual but taking appearance. Soil would not seem to be of much moment in the cultivation of this, or, indeed, the other species of Caragana, for it thrives well either on dry, sunny banks, where the soil is light and thin, or in good, stiff, yellow loam. C. arborescens pendula (1887) only differs in having the branches pendulous.

C. FRUTESCENS.—Siberia, 1752. Flowers in May, and is of partially upright habit; while C. Chamlag, from China, 1773, has greenish-yellow flowers, faintly tinted with pinky-purple.

C. SPINOSA.—Siberia, 1775. This, as the name indicates, is of spiny growth, and is a beautiful and distinct member of the family, with yellow flowers produced in April and May. They are all hardy, and readily propagated from seed.

Cardiandra (Saxifrageæ).

CARDIANDRA ALTERNIFOLIA.—Japan, 1866. With its neat habit, and pretty purple-and-white, plentifully-produced flowers, this is worthy of the small amount of care and coddling required to insure its growth in this country. Hailing from Japan, it cannot be reckoned as very hardy, but treated as a wall plant this pretty evergreen does well and flowers freely. It can, however, be said that it is equally hardy with some of the finer kinds of Hydrangea, to which genus it is nearly allied.

Carpenteria (Saxifrageæ).

Carpenteria californica.—Sierra Nevada, California, 1880. This is undoubtedly one of the most distinct and beautiful of hardy shrubs. That it is perfectly hardy in England and Ireland recently-conducted experiments conclusively prove, as plants have stood unprotected through several unusually severe winters with which this country has of late been visited. When in full bloom the pure-white flowers, resembling those of the Japanese Anemone, render it of great beauty, while the light-grey leaves are of themselves sufficient to make the shrub one of particular attraction. The Carpenteria is nearly related to the Mock Orange (Philadelphus), grows about 10 feet in height, with lithe and slender branches, and broadly lanceolate leaves 2 to 3 inches long. The flowers, which are pure white with a bunch of yellow stamens, and sweet-scented, are produced usually in fives at the branch-tips, and contrast markedly with the long and light green foliage. It grows and flowers with freedom almost anywhere, but is all the better for wall protection. From cuttings or suckers it is readily increased.

Caryopteris (Verbenaceæ).

Caryopteris mastacanthus.—China and Japan, 1844. This is a neat-growing Chinese shrub, 3 or 4 feet high, and of value for its pretty flowers that are produced late in the autumn. It must be ranked as fairly hardy, having stood through the winters of Southern England unprotected; but it is just as well to give so choice a shrub the slight protection afforded by a wall. The leaves are opposite, thickly arranged, and hoary-grey; while the whole plant is twiggy and of strict though by no means formal growth. Flowers lavender-blue or violet, borne in the leaf axils at the tips of the shoots, and appearing in succession for a considerable length of time. Light, sandy peat would seem to suit it well; at least, in such it grows and flowers freely. There is a white-flowered variety.

Cassandra (Ericaceæ). See Andromeda.

CASSANDRA CALYCULATA (*syn Andromeda calyculata*).—North America, 1748. This is a handsome species from the Virginian swamps, but one that is rarely seen in a very satisfactory condition in this country. It grows about 18 inches high, with lanceolate dull-green leaves, and pretty white flowers, individually large and produced abundantly. For the banks of a pond or lake it is a capital shrub and very effective, particularly if massed in groups of from a dozen to twenty plants in each. There are several nursery forms, of which C. calyculata minor is the best and most distinct. Light peaty soil.

Cassia (Leguminosæ).

CASSIA CORYMBOSA.—Buenos Ayres, 1796. A half-hardy shrub that in this country succeeds best when planted against a wall, and in a sheltered, sunny situation. The flowers are both beautiful and conspicuous, being of a showy yellow colour, and, when the plant is established in a suitable site, very freely produced. Sandy peat or leaf-soil seems to suit it well.

Cassinia (Compositæ).

CASSINIA FULVIDA (*syn Diplopappus chrysophyllus*).—New Zealand. This is a neat-growing and beautiful shrub, the rich yellow stems and under sides of the leaves imparting quite a tint of gold to the whole plant. The flowers are individually small, but the whole head, which is creamy-white, is very effective, and contrasts strangely with the golden sheen of this beautiful shrub. It is inclined to be of rather upright growth, is stout and bushy, and is readily increased from cuttings planted in sandy soil in the open border. Probably in the colder parts of the country this charming shrub might not prove perfectly hardy, but all over England and Ireland it seems to be quite at home. The flowers are produced for several months of the year, but are at their best about mid-November, thus rendering the shrub of still further value. It grows freely in sandy peaty soil of a light nature.

Cassiope (Ericaceæ).

CASSIOPE FASTIGIATA (*syn Andromeda fastigiata*) and C. TETRAGONA (*syn Andromeda tetragona*) are small-growing species, only suitable for rock-gardening—the former of neat upright habit, with large pinky-white bells all along the stems; and the latter of bushy growth, with square stems and small white flowers. They succeed best in light peaty soil. C. hypnoides (Lapland, 1798) is of dwarf growth, with reddish-white flowers, and succeeds best in gritty, moist soil.

Castanea (Corylaceæ).

CASTANEA SATIVA (*syn C. vesca* and *C. vulgaris*).—Sweet Spanish Chestnut. Asia Minor. Few persons who have seen this tree as an isolated specimen and when in full flower would feel inclined to exclude it from our list. The long, cylindrical catkins, of a yellowish-green colour, are usually borne in such abundance that the tree is, during the month of June, one of particular interest and beauty.

So common a tree needs no description, but it may be well to mention that there are several worthy varieties, which flower almost equally well with the parent tree.

Catalpa (Bignoniaceæ).

CATALPA BIGNONIOIDES (*syn C. syringæfolia*).—Indian Bean. North America, 1726. When in full bloom this is a remarkable and highly-ornamental tree, the curiously-marked flowers and unusually large, bronzy-tinted foliage being distinct from those of almost any other in cultivation. That it is not, perhaps, perfectly hardy in every part of the country is to be regretted, but the numerous fine old specimens that are to be met with point out that there need be little to fear when assigning this pretty and uncommon tree a position in our parks and gardens. The flowers, produced in spikes at the branch-tips, are white, tinged with violet, and speckled with purple and yellow in the throat. Individually the flowers are of large size and very ornamental, and, being produced freely, give the tree a bright and pleasing appearance when at their best. Usually the tree attains to a height of 30 feet in this country, with rather crooked and ungainly branches, and large heart-shaped leaves that are downy beneath. It flourishes well on any free soil, and is an excellent smoke-resisting tree. C. bignonioides aurea is a decided variety, that differs mainly in the leaves being of a desirable golden tint. There is a good variety named *purpurea*.

C. BUNGEI and C. KAEMPFERI, natives of China and Japan, are hardly to be relied upon, being of tender growth, and, unless in the most favoured situations, suffer from our severe winters. They resemble our commonly cultivated tree.

C. SPECIOSA.—United States, 1879. The Western Catalpa is more erect and taller of growth than C.

bignonioides. The flowers, too, are larger, and of purer white, and with the throat markings of purple and yellow more distinct and not inclined to run into each other. Leaves large, heart-shaped, tapering to a point, of a light pleasing green and soft to the touch. It flowers earlier, and is more hardy than the former.

Ceanothus (Rhamnaceæ).

CEANOTHUS AMERICANUS.—New Jersey Tea. North America, 1713. A shrub of 4 feet in height, with deep green serrated leaves, that are 2 inches long and pubescent on the under sides. Flowers white, in axillary panicles, and produced in great abundance in June. This is one of the hardiest species, but succeeds best when afforded wall protection. C. Americanus variegata (1889) has the leaves bordered with yellow.

C. AZUREUS.—Mexico, 1818. This species, though not hardy enough for every situation, is yet sufficiently so to stand unharmed as a wall plant. It grows from 10 feet to 12 feet high, with deep-green leaves that are hoary on the under sides. The flowers, which are borne in large, axillary panicles, are bright blue, and produced in June and the following months. In a light, dry soil and sunny position, this shrub does well as a wall plant, for which purpose it is one of the most ornamental. There are several good nursery forms, of which the following are amongst the best: C. Azureus Albert Pettitt, C. azureus albidus, C. azureus Arnddii, one of the best, C. azureus Gloire de Versailles, and C. azureus Marie Simon. C. Perle Rose has flowers of a soft, clear, rosy-pink, and is most desirable.

C. CUNEATUS (*syn C. verrucosus*).—California, 1848. This is another half-hardy species that requires wall protection, which may also be said of C. Veitchianus, one of the most beautiful of the family, with dense clusters of rich blue flowers and a neat habit of growth.

C. DENTATUS.—California, 1848. With deeply-toothed, shining-green leaves, and deep-blue, abundantly-produced flowers, this is a well-known wall plant that succeeds in many parts of the country, particularly within the influence of the sea. It commences flowering in May, and frequently continues until frost sets in. It is a very desirable species, that in favoured situations will grow to fully 10 feet high, and with a spread laterally of nearly the same dimensions.

C. PAPILLOSUS.—California, 1848. This is a straggling bush, with small, blunt leaves, and panicles of pale-blue flowers on long footstalks. A native of California and requiring wall protection.

C. RIGIDUS, another Californian species (1848), is of upright, stiff growth, a sub-evergreen, and with deep-purple flowers produced in April and May.

There are other less hardy kinds, including C. floribundus, C. integerrimus, C. velutinus, and C. divaricatus.

Cedrela (Meliaceæ).

CEDRELA SINENSIS (*syn Ailanthus flavescens*).—China, 1875. This is a fast-growing tree, closely resembling the Ailanthus, and evidently quite as hardy. It has a great advantage over that tree, in that the flowers have an agreeable odour, those of the Ailanthus being somewhat sickly and unpleasant. The yellowish flowers are individually small, but arranged in immense hanging bunches like those of Koelreuteria paniculata, and being pleasantly scented are rendered still the more valuable. The whole plant has a yellow hue, and the roots have a peculiar reddish colour, and very unlike those of the Ailanthus, which are white.

Celastrus (Celastrineæ).

Celastrus scandens.—Climbing Waxwork, or Bitter Sweet. North America, 1736. When planted in rich, moist soil, this soon forms an attractive mass of twisting and twining growths, with distinct glossy foliage in summer and brilliant scarlet fruit in autumn. The pale yellow flowers are inconspicuous, the chief beauty of the shrub being the show of fruit, which resembles somewhat that of the Spindle Tree (Euonymus), and to which it is nearly allied. A native of North America, it grows from 12 feet to 15 feet high, and is useful in this country for covering arches or tree stems, or for being allowed to run at will on a mound of earth or on rockwork.

Celtis (Urticaceæ).

Celtis australis.—South Europe, 1796. This species is much like C. occidentalis, with solitary greenish flowers and black edible fruit. It is not of so tall growth as the American species.

C. occidentalis.—Nettle Tree. North America, 1656. In general appearance this tree resembles the Elm, to which family it belongs. It has reticulated, cordate-ovate, serrated leaves, with small, greenish flowers on slender stalks, and succeeded by blackish-purple fruit about the size of a pea. A not very ornamental tree, at least so far as flowers are concerned, but valuable for lawn planting. It varies very much in the size and shape of the leaves.

Cerasus. See Prunus.

Cercis (Leguminosæ).

Cercis canadensis.—North America, 1730. This species resembles C. Siliquastrum, but is of much smaller growth and bears paler flowers; while C. *chinensis* (*syn* C. *japonica*), which is not hardy, has large, rosy-pink flowers.

C. Siliquastrum.—Judas Tree. South Europe, 1596. A small-growing tree of some 15 feet in height, and with usually a rather ungainly and crooked mode of growth. It is, however, one of our choicest subjects for ornamental planting, the handsome reniform leaves and rosy-purple flowers produced along the branches and before the leaves appear rendering it a great favourite with planters. There are three distinct forms of this shrub—the first, C. Siliquastrum alba, having pure-white flowers; C. Siliquastrum carnea, with beautiful deep-pink flowers; and C. Siliquastrum variegata, with neatly variegated foliage, though rather inconstant of character. Natives of South Europe, and amongst the oldest trees of our gardens.

They all succeed best when planted in rather damp loam, and do not object to partial shade, the common species growing well even beneath the drip of large standard trees.

Chimonanthus (Calycanthaceæ).

Chimonanthus fragrans (*syn Calycanthus præcox*).—Winter Flower. Japan, 1766. This Japanese shrub is certainly one of the most remarkable that could be brought under notice, the deliciously-fragrant, whitish-purple flowers being produced in abundance during the winter months, and while the plant is yet leafless. Being of slender growth, it is best suited for planting against a wall, the protection thus afforded being just what is wanted for the perfect development of the pretty flowers. C. fragrans grandiflora has larger and less fragrant flowers than the species, and is more common in cultivation.

Chionanthus (Oleaceæ).

Chionanthus retusus.—China, 1852. This is not a very hardy species, and, being less ornamental than the American form, is not to be recommended for general planting. The flowers, which are white and sweet-scented, are produced in May.

C. virginica.—Fringe Tree. North America, 1796. A very ornamental, small-growing tree, with large deciduous leaves and bearing in June and July pendent clusters of pure-white flowers with long fringe-like petals, and from which the popular name has arisen. In this country it is a charming tree, or rather shrub, for one rarely sees it more than 10 feet high, and one that, to do it justice, must have a cool and rather damp soil and a somewhat shady situation.

Choisya (Rutaceæ).

Choisya ternata.—Mexican Orange Flower. Mexico, 1825. A beautiful and distinct shrub that succeeds well in the South and West of England. The evergreen leaves are always fresh and beautiful, and of a dark, shining green, while the sweetly-fragrant flowers are produced freely on the apices of last year's wood. They have a singular resemblance to those of the orange, and on the Continent are commonly grown as a substitute for that popular flower. The plant succeeds well in any light, rich soil, and soon grows into a goodly-sized shrub of 4 feet or 5 feet in height. As a wall plant it succeeds well, but in warm, maritime situations it may be planted as a standard without fear of harm. Cuttings root freely if placed in slight heat.

Cistus (Cistineæ).

Cistus crispus.—Portugal, 1656. This is a distinct species, with curled leaves, and large, reddish-purple flowers. It is a valuable ornamental shrub, but, like the others, suffers from the effects of frost.

C. LADANIFERUS.—Gum Cistus. Spain, 1629. A pretty but rather tender shrub, growing in favourable situations to about 4 feet in height. It has lanceolate leaves that are glutinous above, and thickly covered with a whitish tomentum on the undersides, and large and showy white flowers with a conspicuous purple blotch at the base of each petal. Unless in Southern and Western England, but particularly on the seacoast, this handsome Portuguese shrub is not to be depended on, in so far as hardihood is concerned.

C. LAURIFOLIUS.—Laurel-leaved Cistus. Spain, 1731. This is the hardiest species in cultivation, but, like the latter, is favourable to the milder parts of these islands, and especially maritime districts. Frequently it rises to 7 feet in height, and is then an object of great beauty, the large, yellowish-white flowers showing well above the deep-green, Laurel-like leaves.

C. MONSPELIENSIS (South of Europe, 1656), and its variety C. monspeliensis florentinus, the former with white, and the latter with white and yellow flowers, are fairly hardy in the milder parts of Britain, but cannot be recommended for general planting.

C. PURPUREUS (LEVANT).—Purple-flowered Cistus. In this species, which may rank next to the latter in point of hardihood, the flowers are of a deep reddish-purple, and with a darker blotch at the base of each petal.

C. SALVIFOLIUS (South Europe, 1548) is of loose and rather untidy growth, with rugose leaves and white flowers. It is very variable in character, and the form generally cultivated grows about 4 feet high, and has ovate-lanceolate, almost glabrous leaves. There are several desirable varieties.

Other species that are occasionally to be found in collections are C. creticus, with yellow and purple flowers; C. hirsutus, white with yellow blotches at the base of the petals; and C. Clusii, with very large, pure-white flowers. All the species of Gum Cistus, or Rock Rose as they are very appropriately named, will be found to succeed best when planted in exalted positions, and light, though rich, strong soil. They are easy of propagation, and self-sown seedlings are not uncommon.

Citharexylum. See Rhaphithamnus.

Citrus (Rutaceæ)

CITRUS TRIFOLIATA.—Japan, 1869. This is a singular low-growing shrub, with ternate leaves, spiny branches, and fragrant white or yellowish flowers. It is hardy in many English situations, but does not fruit freely, although the orange-blossom-like flowers are produced very abundantly. A pretty little glossy-leaved shrub that is well worthy of attention, particularly where a cosy corner can be put aside for its cultivation.

Cladrastis (Leguminosæ).

CLADRASTIS AMURENSIS.—Amoor Yellow Wood. Amoor Valley, 1880. This is a shrub that is sure to be extensively cultivated when better known, and more readily procured. It has stood uninjured for several years in various parts of England, so that its hardihood may be taken for granted. The pretty olive-green of the bark, and the greyish-green of the leathery leaves, render the shrub one of interest even in a flowerless state. In July and August the dense spikes of white, or rather yellowish-white, flowers are produced freely, and that, too, even before the shrub has attained to a height of 2 feet. It is well worthy of extended culture.

C. TINCTORIA (*syn C. lutea* and *Virgilia lutea*).—Yellow Wood. North America, 1812. This is a handsome deciduous tree that does well in many parts of the country, and is valued for the rich profusion of white flowers produced, and which are well set off by the finely-cut pinnate leaves It is a valuable tree for park and lawn planting, requiring a warm, dry soil, and sunny situation—conditions under which the wood becomes well-ripened, and the flowers more freely produced.

Clematis (Ranunculaceæ).

CLEMATIS ALPINA (*syn Atragene alpina, A. austriaca* and *A. sibirica*).—Europe and North America, 1792. This is a climbing species with bi-ternately divided leaves, and large flowers with four blue sepals and ten to twelve small flattened organs, which are usually termed petals.

C. CIRRHOSA.—Evergreen Virgin's Bower. Spain, 1596. An interesting, early-flowering species. The flowers, which are greenish-white, are produced in bunches and very effective. It is an evergreen species, of comparative hardihood, and flowers well in sheltered situations.

C. FLAMMULA.—Virgin's Bower. France, 1596. An old and well-known plant that is quite hardy in this country. The leaves are pinnate, and the flowers white and fragrant, and produced from May to October. C. Flammula rubro-marginata is a worthy and beautiful-leaved variety.

C. FLORIDA.—Japan, 1776. This is a beautiful species, and an old inhabitant of English gardens. Leaves composed of usually three oval-shaped leaflets, and unusually bright of tint. The flowers are very large, and pure white. It should be planted in a warm, sheltered corner against a wall.

C. GRAVEOLENS.—This is a dwarf shrub, with neatly tripinnate leaves, and solitary, strongly-scented yellow flowers of medium size. A native of Chinese Tartary, and introduced in 1844. Quite hardy.

C. HAKONENSIS.—Japan, 1860. This is a vigorous twiner with violet-purple flowers, each about 6 inches in diameter, produced from July to October. The well-known and justly popular C. Jackmanni, of gardens, is a variety.

C. LANUGINOSA.—China, 1851. A handsome species,

with large purple leaves that are hairy on the undersides. Flowers pale blue or lilac, very large, and composed of six or eight spreading sepals. C. lanuginosa pallida has immense flowers, often fully half a foot in diameter. Flowers in June.

C. MONTANA.—Nepaul, 1831. This is valuable on account of its flowering in May. It is a free-growing species, with trifoliolate leaves on long footstalks, and large white flowers. C. montana grandiflora is a beautiful variety, having large white flowers so abundantly produced as to hide the foliage. It is quite hardy and of rampant growth.

C. PATENS (*syns C. cærulea* and *C. azurea grandiflora*).—Japan, 1836. This has large, pale-violet flowers, and is the parent of many single and double flowered forms. The typical form is, however, very deserving of cultivation, on account of the freedom with which it blooms during June and July from the wood of the previous year. It is perfectly hardy even in the far north.

C. VIORNA.—Leather Flower. United States, 1730. This is a showy, small-flowered species, the flowers being campanulate, greenish-white within and purplish without. C. Viorna coccinea is not yet well known, but is one of the prettiest of the small-flowered section. The flowers, which are leathery as in the species, are of a beautiful vermilion on the outside and yellow within.

C. VITALBA.—Lady's Bower, or Old Man's Beard. A handsome native climbing shrub, common in limestone or chalky districts, and unusually abundant in the southern English counties. Clambering over some neglected fence, often to nearly 20 feet in height, this vigorous-growing plant is seen to best advantage, the three- or five-lobed leaves and festoons of greenish-white, fragrant flowers, succeeded by the curious and attractive feathery carpels, rendering the plant one of the most distinct and desirable of our native wildlings flowering in August.

C. Viticella.—Spain, 1569. This is a well-known species of not too rampant growth, and a native of Spain and Italy. The flowers vary a good deal in colour, but in the typical plant they are reddish-purple and produced throughout the summer. Crossed with C. lanuginosa, this species has produced many ornamental and beautiful hybrids. There is a double-flowered variety.

C. Williamsi (*syn C. Fortunei*).—Japan, 1863. The fragrant white flowers of this species are semi-double, and consist of about a hundred oblong-lanceolate sepals narrowed to the base. The leathery leaves are trifoliolate with heart-shaped leaflets. It proves quite hardy, and has several varieties.

Garden Varieties.—As well as the above there are many beautiful garden hybrids, some of which in point of floral colouring far outvie the parent forms. Included in the following list are a few of the most beautiful kinds :—

Albert Victor.
Alexandra.
Beauty of Worcester.
Belle of Woking.
Blue Gem.
Duchess of Albany.
Duchess of Edinburgh.
Edith Jackman.
Fairy Queen.
Imperatrice Eugénie.
John Gould Veitch.
Lady Bovill.
Lilacina floribunda.
Lord Beaconsfield.
Lucie Lemoine.
Madame Baron Veillard.
Miss Bateman.
Mrs. A. Jackman.
Othello.
Prince of Wales.
Rubella.
Star of India.
Stella.
Venus Victrix.
William Kennett.

The Clematis is by no means particular as to soil, and succeeds and flowers freely in light, rich loam that is well drained.

Clerodendron (Verbenaceæ).

Clerodendron fœtidum.—China, 1820. This is only hardy in southern and seaside situations, where it forms a bush 5 feet high, armed with sharp, rigid prickles, and dark-green, heart-shaped, deciduous leaves, which are downy on both surfaces, and large clusters of rosy-pink flowers.

C. trichotomum.—Japan, 1800. This is at once one of the most beautiful and distinct of hardy shrubs. It is of stout, nearly erect growth, 8 feet high, and about as much through, with large, dark-green, ovate leaves, and dense corymbs of deliciously fragrant white flowers, with a purplish calyx, which are at their best in September. Thriving well in any light soil, being of vigorous constitution, and extremely handsome of flower, are qualities which combine to render this shrub one of particular importance in our gardens.

Clethra (Ericaceæ).

Clethra acuminata.—Pointed-leaved Pepper Tree. Carolina, 1806. This is not so hardy as C. alnifolia, hailing from the Southern States of North America, but with a little protection is able to do battle with our average English winter. It resembles C. alnifolia, except in the leaves, which are sharp-pointed, and, like that species, delights to grow in damp positions. The flowers are white and drooping, and the growth more robust than is that of C. alnifolia generally. For planting by the pond or lake-side, the Pepper Trees are almost invaluable.

C. alnifolia.—Alder-leaved Pepper Tree. North America, 1731. A rather stiff-growing shrub about 5 feet in height, with leaves resembling those of our common Alder, and bearing towards the end of July spikes of almost oppressively fragrant dull-white flowers at the tips of the branches. It is a valuable shrub, not only in an ornamental way, but on account of its thriving in damp, swampy ground, where few others could exist, while at the same time it will succeed and flower freely in almost any good garden soil.

Cleyera (Ternströmiaceæ).

CLEYERA JAPONICA.—Japan, 1820. This is a variable species, with oblong-lanceolate, evergreen leaves, and small, whitish-yellow, fragrant flowers. There is a variegated variety in which the leaf-margins are of a pale yellow colour. In light soil and a warm situation it does well, but cannot be recommended for general planting.

Clianthus (Leguminosæ).

CLIANTHUS PUNICEUS.—New Zealand, 1832. A shrubby plant, the foliage of which is covered with silky hairs, and produces abundantly scarlet, boat-shaped flowers. With the protection of a wall it flowers freely in the warmer parts of this country, when planted in any light, rich soil.

Cocculus (Menispermaceæ).

COCCULUS CAROLINUS.—United States. This is a half-hardy, twining shrub, of free growth when planted by a tree stem in a sheltered wood, but with by no means showy greenish flowers; indeed, it may be described in few words as a shrub of no great beauty nor value.

C. LAURIFOLIUS, from the Himalayas and Japan, 1820, is even less hardy than the above, although, used as a wall plant, it has survived for many years in the South and West of England. The foliage of this species is neat and ornamental, but liable to injury from cold easterly winds, while the flowers are whitish-green.

Colletia (Rhamneæ).

Colletia cruciata (*syn C. bictonensis*).—Chili, 1824. With flattened woody branches, and sharp-pointed spines which take the place of leaves, this is at once one of the most singular of hardy flowering shrubs. It forms a stout, dense bush about 4 feet high, and bears quantities of small, white flowers, which render the plant one of great beauty during the summer months.

C. spinosa.—Peru, 1823. This species grows fairly well in some parts of England and Ireland, and is a curious shrub with awl-shaped leaves, and, like the other members of the family, an abundant producer of flowers. It thrives best as a wall plant, and when favourably situated a height of 12 feet is sometimes attained. Light, loamy soil suits the Colletias.

Colutea (Leguminosæ).

Colutea arborescens.—Bladder Senna. France, 1568. This is a common plant in English gardens, bearing yellow, Pea-shaped flowers, that are succeeded by curious, reddish, bladder-like seed-pods. It grows to 10 feet or 12 feet in height, and is usually of lax and slender growth, but perfectly hardy. A good town plant, and one that is by no means particular about the soil in which it is planted. C. arborescens melanocalyx (Asia Minor, 1892) is a desirable variety.

C. cruenta (*syn C. orientalis and C. sanguinea*).—Oriental Bladder Senna. Levant, 1731. This is a free-growing, round-headed, deciduous bush, of from 6 feet to 8 feet high when fully grown. The leaves are pinnate and glaucous, smooth, and bright green above, and downy beneath. Flowers individually large, of a reddish-copper colour, with a yellow spot at the base of the upper petal. The fruit is an inflated, boat-shaped, reddish pod. The

Bladder Sennas are of very free growth, even in poor, sandy soil, and being highly ornamental, whether in flower or fruit, are to be recommended for extensive cultivation.

Comptonia. See Myrica.

Corchorus. See Kerria.

Coriaria (Coriarieæ).

Coriaria myrtifolia.—South Europe, 1629. A deciduous shrub growing to about 4 feet in height, with Myrtle-like leaves, and upright terminal racemes of not very showy flowers, produced about mid-summer—generally from May to August. For its pretty foliage and the frond-like arrangement of its branches it is principally worthy of culture. From Southern Europe and the North of Africa, where it is an occupant of waste ground and hedges, but still rare in our gardens.

Cornus (Cornaceæ).

Cornus alba.—White-fruited Dogwood. Siberia, 1741. This is a native of Northern Asia and Siberia, not of America, as Loudon stated. For the slender, red-barked branches and white or creamy flowers, this species is well worthy of notice, while the white fruit renders it very distinct and effective. It grows to about 10 feet in height. C. alba Spathi is one of the most ornamental of shrubs bearing coloured leaves, these in spring being of a beautiful bronzy tint, and changing towards summer to a mixture of gold and green, or rather an irregular margin of deep gold surrounds each leaf. It was first sent out by the famous Berlin nurseryman whose name it bears. C. alba Gouchaulti is another variegated leaved variety, but has no particular merit, and originated in one of the French nurseries. Both varieties have been referred to C. tartarica by some writers.

C. ALTERNIFOLIA.—North America, 1760. This species is a lover of damp ground, and grows from 20 feet to nearly 30 feet high, with clusters of pale-yellow flowers, succeeded by bluish-black berries that render the plant highly ornamental. It is still rare in British gardens.

C. AMOMUM (*syn C. sericea*).—From the eastern United States, 1683. It is a low-growing, damp-loving shrub, with yellowish-white flowers, borne abundantly in small clusters. It grows about 8 feet in height, and has a graceful habit, owing to the long and lithe branches spreading regularly over the ground. The fruit is pale blue, and the bark a conspicuous purple.

C. ASPERIFOLIA is another showy American species, with reddish-brown bark, hairy leaves, of small size, and rather small flowers that are succeeded by pearly-white berries borne on conspicuous reddish stalks.

C. BAILEYI resembles somewhat the better-known C. stolonifera, but it is of more erect habit, is not stoloniferous, has rather woolly leaves, at least on the underside, and bears yellowish-white fruit. It grows in sandy soil, and is a native of Canada.

C. CALIFORNICA (*syn C. pubescens*) grows fully 10 feet high, with smooth branches, hairy branchlets, and cymes of pretty white flowers, succeeded by white fruit. It occurs from Southern California to British Columbia.

C. CANADENSIS.—Dwarf Cornel or Birchberry. Canada, 1774. This is of herbaceous growth, and remarkable for the large, cream-coloured flower bracts, and showy, red fruit.

C. CANDIDISSIMA (*syn C. paniculata*) is a beautiful American species, with panicled clusters of almost pure-white flowers, that are succeeded by pale-blue fruit. It is a small-growing tree, with narrow, pointed leaves, and greyish coloured, smooth bark. Like many of its fellows, this species likes rather moist ground.

C. CIRCINATA, from the eastern United States, is readily distinguished by its large, round leaves, these sometimes measuring 6 inches long by 3½ inches wide. The yellowish-white flowers are individually small, and succeeded by bright-blue fruits, each as large as a pea. There are two varieties, variegata and elegantissima.

C. CAPITATA (*syn Benthamia fragifera*).—Nepaul, 1825. An evergreen shrub, with oblong, light-green leaves and terminal, inconspicuous, greenish flowers, surrounded by an involucre of four large, pinky-yellow bracts. It is this latter that renders the shrub so very conspicuous when in full flower. Unfortunately, this species is not hardy throughout the country, the South and West of England, especially Cornwall, and the southern parts of Ireland being the favoured spots where this handsome shrub or small-growing tree—for in Cornwall it has attained to fully 45 feet in height, and in Cork nearly 30 feet—may be found in a really thriving condition. Around London it does well enough for a time, but with severe frost it gets cut back to the ground, and though it quickly recovers and grows rapidly afterwards, before it is large enough to flower freely it usually suffers again. The fruits are as large as and resemble Strawberries, and are of a rich scarlet or reddish hue, and though ripe in October they frequently remain on the trees throughout the winter. Both for its flowers and fruit, this Nepaul shrub-tree is well worthy of a great amount of trouble to get it established in a cosy corner of the garden. Rich, well-drained loam is all it wants, while propagation by seed is readily effected.

C. FLORIDA.—United States, 1731. The Florida Dogwood is not always very satisfactory when grown in this country, our climate in some way or other being unsuitable for its perfect development. It is a handsome shrub or small-growing tree, with small flowers surrounded by a large and conspicuous white involucre. The leaves are ovate-oblong, and pubescent on the undersides. It is a valuable as well as ornamental little tree, and is worthy of a great amount of coddling and coaxing to get it established. There is a red-flowered variety, C. florida rubra.

C. Kousa (*syn Benthamia japonica*).—Japan, 1847. This is a very distinct and beautiful flowering shrub. Flowers very small individually, but borne in large clusters, and yellow, the showy part being the four large, pure-white bracts which subtend each cluster of blossoms, much like those in Cornus florida, only the bracts are more pointed than those of the latter species. Being quite hardy, and a plant of great interest and beauty, this little-known Cornus is sure to be widely planted when better known.

C. macrophylla (*syn C. brachypoda*).—Himalayas, China, and Japan, 1827. This is an exceedingly handsome species, of tabulated appearance, occasioned by the branches being arranged almost horizontally. The leaves are of large size, elliptic-ovate, and are remarkable for their autumnal tints. The elder-like flowers appear in June. They are pure white and arranged in large cymes. C. macrophylla variegata is a distinct and very ornamental form of the above, in which the leaf margins are bordered with white.

C. Mas.—Cornelian Cherry. Austria, 1596. One of our earliest flowering trees, the clusters of yellow blooms being produced in mild seasons by the middle of February. It is not at all fastidious about soil, thriving well in those of very opposite description. It deserves to be extensively cultivated, if only for the profusion of brightly-tinted flowers, which completely cover the shoots before the leaves have appeared. C. Mas aurea-elegantissima, the tricolour-leaved Dogwood, is a strikingly ornamental shrub, with green leaves encircled with a golden band, the whole being suffused with a faint pinky tinge. It is of more slender growth than the species, and a very desirable acquisition to any collection of hardy ornamental shrubs.

C. Mas argenteo-variegata is another pretty shrub, the leaves being margined with clear white.

C. NUTTALLI grows to fully 50 feet in height, and is one of the most beautiful of the Oregon and Californian forest trees. The flower bracts are of large size, often 6 inches across, the individual bracts being broad and white, and fully 2½ inches long.

C. OFFICINALIS is a Japanese species, that is, however, quite hardy in this country, and nearly resembles the better-known C. Mas, but from which it may at once be known by the tufts of brownish hairs that are present in the axils of the principal leaf veins.

C. SANGUINEA.—Britain. A native shrub that is valued for its colouring of bark, which is of the brightest red, and most effective during the winter season. The flowers are plentifully produced and of a creamy-white colour, while the leaves are ovate and opposite. The pretty black berries are a feature of the shrub in winter. Dampish loam.

C. STOLONIFERA.—Red Osier Dogwood. North America, 1741. This has rather inconspicuous flowers, that are succeeded by whitish fruit, and is of greatest value for the ruddy tint of the young shoots. It grows fully 6 feet high, and increases rapidly by underground suckers. This species is quite hardy.

C. TARTARICA (*syn C. sibirica*).—Siberia, 1824. This has much brighter coloured bark, and is of neater and dwarfer habit, than the typical C. alba. It is a very beautiful and valuable shrub, of which there is a variegated leaved and other varieties. Light, rich, dampish loam suits the Cornus well.

Corokia (Cornaceæ).

COROKIA COTONEASTER.—New Zealand, 1876. A curious, low, rigid, dwarf-growing shrub, with small, sweet-scented, bright yellow, starry flowers produced in June. The hardiness of the shrub is rather doubtful.

Coronilla (Leguminosæ).

Coronilla Emerus.—Scorpion Senna. France, 1596. This shrub, a native of the middle and southern parts of Europe, forms an elegant loose bush about 5 feet high, with smooth, pinnate, sub-evergreen leaves, and Pea-shaped flowers, that are reddish in the bud state, but bright yellow when fully expanded. It is an elegant plant, and on account of its bearing hard cutting back, is well suited for ornamental hedge formation; but however used the effect is good, the distinct foliage and showy flowers making it a general favourite with planters. It will thrive in very poor soil, but prefers a light, rich loam.

Corylopsis (Hamamelideæ).

Corylopsis Himalayana.—E. Himalayas, 1879. This is a stronger growing species than C. pauciflora or C. spicata, with large leaves averaging 4 inches long, that are light green above and silky on the undersides. The parallel veins of the leaves are very pronounced, while the leaf-stalks, as, indeed, the young twigs too, are covered with a hairy pubescence. The flowers are yellowish-white.

C. pauciflora, from Japan, is readily distinguished from the former by its more slender growth, smaller leaves, and fewer flowered spikes. Flowers primrose-yellow.

C. spicata.—Japan, 1864. This Japanese shrub is of very distinct appearance, having leaves like those of our common Hazel, and drooping spikes of showy-yellowish, fragrant flowers that are produced before the leaves. There is a variegated form in cultivation.

The various species of Corylopsis are very ornamental garden plants, and to be recommended, on account of their early flowering, for prominent positions in the shrubbery or by the woodland walk. Light, rich loam seems to suit them well.

Corylus (Corylaceæ).

Corylus Avellana purpurea.—Purple Hazel. This has large leaves of a rich purple colour, with crimson flowers, and is a very distinct and ornamental plant for the shrubbery border. It should be cut down annually if large leaves are desired.

C. Avellana aurea has rich golden foliage, while C. Avellana laciniata has the leaves neatly cut, and C. Avellana pendula is a weeping variety, but of no particular value for ornamental planting.

C. Colurna.—Constantinople Hazel. Turkey, 1665. This is the largest and most ornamental of the family, and is mentioned here on account of the showy catkins with which the tree is well supplied. When thickly produced, as they usually are on established specimens, these long catkins have a most effective and pleasing appearance, and tend to render the tree one of the most distinct in cultivation. Under favourable circumstances, such as when growing in a sweet and rather rich brown loam, it attains to fully 60 feet in height, and is of neat shape, from the branches being arranged horizontally, or nearly so. Even in a young state the Constantinople Hazel is readily distinguished from the common English species, by the softer and more angular leaves, and by the whitish bark which comes off in long strips. The stipules, too, form an unerring guide to its identity, they being long, linear, and recurved. All the Hazels succeed in rich, dampish loam.

Cotoneaster (Rosaceæ).

Cotoneaster bacillaris.—Nepaul, 1841. A large-growing deciduous species, and one of the few members of the family that is more ornamental when in flower than in fruit. It is of bold, portly, upright growth, and sends up shoots from the base of the plant. The pretty white flowers are borne in clusters for some distance along the slender shoots, and are very effective and pleasing; indeed, the upper portion of the plant has the appearance of a mass of white blossoms.

C. FRIGIDA.—Nepaul, 1824. This species forms a large shrub or low tree with oblong, elliptical, sub-evergreen leaves. The flowers are white and borne in large corymbs during April and May, these being succeeded by an abundance of scarlet berries in September.

C. MICROPHYLLA.—Small-leaved Cotoneaster. Nepaul, 1824. This is, from a flowering point of view, probably the most useful of any member of this rather large genus. Its numerous pretty white flowers, dark, almost Yew-green leaves, and abundance of the showiest red berries in winter, will ever make this dwarf, clambering plant a favourite with those who are at all interested in beautiful shrubs.

C. PANNOSA.—Yunnan, 1898. A desirable and rare species that is of the readiest culture. It is of refined growth, growing about 5 feet high, with ovate-oblong leaves that are fully an inch long, and a plentiful supply of small white flowers that are borne in corymbs, and are succeeded by bright-red berries.

C. SIMONSII.—Khasia, 1868. The stems of this species usually grow from 4 feet to 6 feet high, and are of sub-erect habit. The leaves are roundly-elliptic and slightly silky beneath. The small flowers are succeeded by a profusion of scarlet berries that ripen in autumn. This is generally considered the best for garden purposes, and is evergreen in mild winters.

All, or nearly all, the species of Cotoneaster are remarkable and highly valued for their showy berries, but, except the above, and, perhaps, C. buxifolia (Box-leaved Cotoneaster), C. thymifolia (Himalayas, 1852), with small pinky flowers, C. multiflora (Cashmir, 1837) and C. congesta (Himalayas, 1868), both with white flowers, few others are worthy of consideration from a purely flowering point of view. Any free, light soil will suit the Cotoneasters.

Cratægus (Rosaceæ).

CRATÆGUS AZAROLUS.—South Europe, 1640. This is a very vigorous-growing species, with a wide, spreading head of rather upright-growing branches. The flowers are showy, white and sweet-scented, and the fruit large and of a pleasing red colour.

C. AZAROLUS ARONIA (*syn C. Aronia* and *C. maura*).—Aronia Thorn. South Europe, 1810. This tree attains to a height of 20 feet, has deeply-lobed leaves that are wedge-shaped at the base, and slightly pubescent on the undersides. The flowers, which are usually at their best in June, are white and showy, and succeeded by large, yellow fruit. Generally the Aronia Thorn forms a rather upright and branchy specimen of neat proportions, and when studded with its milk-white flowers may be included amongst the most distinct and ornamental of the family.

C. COCCINEA.—Scarlet-fruited Thorn. North America, 1683. If only for its lovely white flowers, with bright, pinky anthers, it is well worthy of a place even in a selection of ornamental flowering trees and shrubs. It is, however, rendered doubly valuable in that the cordate-ovate leaves turn of a warm brick colour in the autumn, while the fruit, which is usually produced abundantly, is of the brightest red.

C. COCCINEA MACRANTHA.—North America, 1819. This bears some resemblance to the Cockspur Thorn, but has very long, curved spines—longer, perhaps, than those of any other species. There are other varieties, including corallina, glandulosa, indentata, maxima, and minor.

C. CORDATA (United States, 1738) is one of the latest flowering species, in which respect it is even more decided than the well-known C. tanacetifolia. It forms a small, compact tree, of neat and regular outline, with dark-green shining leaves, and deep-red berries about the same size as those of the common species.

C. CRUS-GALLI.—Cockspur Thorn. North America, 1691. This has large and showy white flowers that are succeeded by deep-red berries. It is readily distinguished by the long, curved spines with which the whole tree is beset. Of this species there are numerous worthy forms, including C. Crus-galli Carriere, which opens at first white, and then turns a showy flesh colour; C. Crus-galli linearis, C. Crus-galli splendens, C. Crus-galli prunifolia, C. Crus-galli pyracanthifolia, and C. Crus-galli salicifolia, all forms of great beauty—whether for their foliage, or showy and usually plentifully-produced flowers.

C. DOUGLASII.—North America, 1827. This is peculiar in having dark purple or almost black fruit. It is of stout growth, often reaching to 20 feet in height, with rigid spines, and belongs to the early-flowering section. The flowers are white, and produced in May.

C. NIGRA (*syn C. carpatica*).—Eastern Europe, 1819. A tree 20 feet high, with stout branches, and downy, spineless shoots. Leaves large, ovate-acute, deeply incised, glossy green above and downy beneath. Flowers large and fragrant, pure white, and produced in close heads in June. Fruit large, oval, downy, and yellowish-black when fully ripe. This species must not be confused with a variety of our common Thorn bearing a similar name.

C. OXYACANTHA.—Common Hawthorn. This is, perhaps, the most ornamental species in cultivation, and certainly the commonest. The common wild species needs no description, the fragrant flowers, varying in colour from pure white to pink, being produced in the richest profusion. Under cultivation, however, it has produced some very distinct and desirable forms, far superior to the parent, including amongst others those with double-white, pink, and scarlet flowers.

C. Oxyacantha punicea flore-pleno (Paul's double-scarlet Thorn) is one of, if not the handsomest variety, with large, double flowers that are of the richest crimson. Other good flowering kinds include C. Oxyacantha præcox (Glastonbury Thorn); C. Oxyacantha Oliveriana; C. Oxyacantha punicea, with deep-scarlet flowers; C. Oxyacantha rosea, rose-coloured and abundantly-produced flowers; C. Oxyacantha foliis aureis, with yellow fruit; C. Oxyacantha laciniata, cut leaves; C. Oxyacantha multiplex, double-white flowers; C. Oxyacantha foliis argenteis, having silvery-variegated leaves; C. Oxyacantha pendula, of semi-weeping habit; C. Oxyacantha stricta, with an upright and stiff habit of growth; C. Oxyacantha Leeana, a good form; and C. Oxyacantha leucocarpa.

C. PARVIFOLIA.—North America, 1704. This is a miniature Thorn, of slow growth, with leaves about an inch long, and solitary pure white flowers of large size, which open late in the season, and are succeeded by yellowish-green fruit.

C. PYRACANTHA.—Fiery Thorn. South Europe, 1629. This is a very distinct species, with lanceolate serrated evergreen leaves, and pinkish or nearly white flowers. The berries of this Thorn are, however, the principal attraction, being orange-scarlet, and produced in dense clusters. C. Pyracantha crenulata and C. Pyracantha Lelandi are worthy varieties of the above, the latter especially being one of the most ornamental-berried shrubs in cultivation.

C. TANACETIFOLIA.—Tansy-leaved Thorn. Greece, 1789. This is a very late-flowering species, and remarkable for its Tansy-like foliage. It is of unusually free growth in almost any class of soil, and is undoubtedly, in so far at least as neatly divided leaves and wealth of fruit are concerned, one of the most distinct and desirable species of Thorn. The white flowers are produced in May.

Other good species and varieties that may just be mentioned as being worthy of cultivation are C. apiifolia,

C. Crus-galli horrida, C. orientalis, and C. tomentosum (*syn C. punctata*). To a lesser or greater extent, the various species and varieties of Thorn are of great value for the wealth and beauty of flowers they produce, but the above are, perhaps, the most desirable in that particular respect. They are all of free growth, and, except in waterlogged soils, thrive well and flower freely.

Cydonia. See Pyrus.

Cytisus (Leguminosæ). See Genista, Spartium, and Laburnum.

CYTISUS ALBUS.—White Spanish Broom. Portugal, 1752. This is a large-growing shrub of often 10 feet in height, with wiry, somewhat straggling branches, and remarkable for the wealth of pure-white flowers it produces. In May and June, if favourably situated, every branch is wreathed with small white flowers, and often to such an extent that at a short distance away the plant looks like a sheet of white. Being perfectly hardy and of very free growth in any light soil, and abundantly floriferous, this handsome shrub is one of particular value in ornamental planting. By placing three or five plants in clump-fashion, the beauty of this Broom is greatly enhanced.

C. ALBUS INCARNATUS (*syn C. incarnatus*) resembles C. purpureus in its leaves and general appearance, but it is of larger growth. The flowers, which are at their best in May, are of a vinous-rose colour, and produced plentifully.

C. ARDOINI, from the maritime Alps, 1867, is a charming rock shrub with decumbent stems, hairy leaves, and bright-yellow flowers.

C. BIFLORUS (*syn C. elongatus*).—Hungary, 1760. This is a dwarf, spreading, twiggy bush, of fully a yard in height. Leaves trifoliate, clothed beneath with closely adpressed hairs, and bright-yellow, somewhat tubular flowers, usually produced in fours.

C. DECUMBENS (*syn Genista prostrata*).—A charming alpine species, of low, spreading growth, with bright-green, three-parted leaves, and bearing axillary bunches of large yellow, brownish-purple-tinted flowers. A native of the French and Italian Alps, and quite hardy.

C. KEWENSIS is of remarkably prostrate habit with creamy-white flowers, and is a cross between C. albus and C. Ardoini, and was raised at Kew.

C. NIGRICANS.—Austria, 1730. Another beautiful species, with long, erect racemes of golden-yellow flowers, and one whose general hardihood is undoubted. On its own roots, and allowed to roam at will, this pretty, small-growing Broom is of far greater interest than when it is grafted mop-high on a Laburnum stem, and pruned into artificial shapes, as is, unfortunately, too often the case.

C. PURPUREUS.—Purple Broom. Austria, 1792. A beautiful low, spreading shrub, with long, wiry shoots, clothed with neat trifoliate leaves, and bearing an abundance of purple, Pea-shaped flowers. There is a white-flowered form, C. purpureus albus, and another named C. purpureus ratisbonensis, with pretty yellow flowers, produced on long and slender shoots.

C. SCOPARIUS.—Yellow Broom. This is a well-known native shrub, with silky, angular branches, and bright-yellow flowers in summer. There are several varieties, but the most remarkable and handsome is C. scoparius Andreanus, in which the wings of the flowers are of a rich golden brown. It is one of the showiest shrubs in cultivation, and was found wild in Normandy in 1886.

C. SCHIPKÆNSIS (Balkan Mountains, 1892) is a worthy species with plentifully-produced white flowers. Of hybrid forms there are many, such as *præcox*, with wreaths of sulphur-yellow flowers produced early in the season. The parents are C. purgans and C. albus.

For ornamental planting the above are about the best forms of Broom, but others might include C. austriacus (East Europe, 1731) and C. capitatus (Europe, 1774), the latter being unusually hardy, and bearing dense heads of yellowish flowers. In so far as soil is concerned, the Brooms are readily accommodated, that of a light nature being preferred, while either from seeds or cuttings they are easily propagated.

Daboecia (Ericaceæ). See Menziesia.

DABŒCIA POLIFOLIA (*syn Menziesia polifolia*).—St. Dabeoc's Heath. South-Western Europe, Ireland, and the Azores. A dwarf, and rather straggling, viscid shrub, with linear-ovate leaves that are silvery beneath. The elegant drooping flowers are pink, and abundantly produced. D. polifolia alba has white flowers; D. polifolia atro-purpurea, purplish flowers; while D. polifolia calyculata has red and white flowers. Sandy peat will suit their wants.

Danæ (Liliaceæ). See Ruscus.

DANÆ LAURUS (*syn D. racemosa* and *Ruscus racemosus*).—Alexandrian Laurel. A native of Portugal (1739), with glossy-green leaf substitutes, and racemes of small, not very showy, greenish-yellow flowers. Rich, light loam suits it well.

Daphne (Thymelaceæ).

DAPHNE ALPINA.—Italy, 1759. A desirable species, which has white or rosy-white, sweet-scented flowers. It is a pretty, but rare shrub, that grows well in light, sandy leaf-soil.

D. ALTAICA.—Siberia, 1796. Though rare in gardens, this is a pretty and neat-foliaged species, and bears white scentless flowers in abundance. It wants a warm corner and dry soil.

D. Blagayana.—Styria, 1872. This is still rare in cultivation, but it is a very desirable evergreen species, bearing ivory-white highly-fragrant flowers. For the alpine garden it is particularly suitable, and though growing rather slowly thrives well in good light soil.

D. cneorum.—Garland Flower. South Europe, 1752. This is a charming rock shrub, of dwarf, trailing habit, with small, glossy-green leaves, and dense clusters of bright - pink, deliciously - fragrant flowers. There are several forms.

D. Fioniana is of neat growth, with small, glossy, dark leaves, and pale rose-coloured flowers. Its sturdy, dwarf habit, constant verdure, and pretty sweet-scented flowers, should make this species a favourite with cultivators. Known also as D. hyemalis.

D. Fortunei, from China, 1844, is a rare and pretty species, bearing lilac flowers in winter, and whilst the shrub is leafless. It does best in a warm situation, such as planted against a wall facing south.

D. Genkwa.—Japanese Lilac. Japan, 1866. This is a rare and beautiful species, about a yard high, with large, lilac-tinted, sweetly-scented flowers, appearing before the leaves.

D. glomerata (Caucasus, 1891) is a dwarf, hardy species, with oval lanceolate leaves an inch long, and umbels of violet-purple flowers.

D. Laureola.—Spurge Laurel. This is not, in so far at least as flowers are concerned, a showy species, but the ample foliage and sturdy habit of the plant will always render it an acquisition for the shrubbery. It is of value, too, as growing and flowering freely in the shade. The flowers are sweetly scented, of a greenish-yellow colour, and appear about February.

D. Mezereum.—The Mezereon. Europe (England). One of the commonest and most popular of hardy garden shrubs. It is of stout, strict growth, and produces clusters of pinky, rose, or purplish flowers before winter is past, and while the branches are yet leafless. Few perfectly hardy flowering shrubs are so popular as the Mezereon, and rightly so, for a more beautiful plant could not be mentioned, wreathed as every branch is, and almost back to the main stem, with the showiest of flowers. It likes good, rich, dampish soil, and delights to grow in a quiet, shady nook, or even beneath the spread of our larger forest trees. There are several very distinct varieties, of which the white-flowered D. Mezereum flore albo is one of the most valuable. The fruit of this variety is bright golden-yellow. D. Mezereum autumnale and D. Mezereum atro-rubrum are likewise interesting and beautiful forms.

D. PETRÆA (*syn D. rupestris*).—Rock Daphne. Tyrol. This is quite hardy in the more sheltered corners of the rock garden, with neat, shining foliage and pretty rosy flowers, produced so thickly all over the plant as almost to hide the foliage from view. At Kew it thrives well in peaty loam and limestone, and although it does not increase very quickly is yet happy and contented. It is a charming rock shrub.

D. PONTICA.—Pontic Daphne. Asia Minor, 1759. This is much like D. laureola, but has shorter and more oval leaves, and the flowers, instead of being borne in fives like that species, are produced in pairs. They are also a richer yellow, and more sweetly scented.

D. SERICEA (*syn D. collina*).—Italy and Asia Minor, 1820. This forms a bush fully 2 feet high, with evergreen, oblong, shining leaves, and clusters of rose-coloured flowers that are pleasantly scented, and produced in April and May. It is quite hardy, and an interesting species that is well worthy of more extended culture. There is a variety of this with broader foliage than the species, and named D. sericea latifolia (*syn D. collina latifolia*). The Daphnes should be transplanted in autumn, the soil best suited being that of a cool, moist, loamy description.

Daphniphyllum (Euphorbiaceæ).

DAPHNIPHYLLUM GLAUCESCENS (*syn D. macropodum*).—East Indies, Java, and Corea. A handsome Japanese shrub that will be valued for its neat Rhododendron-like foliage, compact habit of growth, and for the conspicuous bark, which is of a warm reddish hue. The leaves are large and elliptic, 6 inches long, and are rendered strangely conspicuous from the foot-stalks and midrib being dull crimson, this affording a striking contrast to the delicate green of the leaves. It grows freely in light, sandy peat. There are two well-marked forms, one named D. glaucescens viridis, in which the red markings of the leaves are absent; and D. glaucescens jezoense, a pretty and uncommon variety.

Desfontainea (Loganiaceæ).

DESFONTAINEA SPINOSA.—Andes from Chili to New Grenada, 1853. This is a desirable and the only species, and one that is perfectly hardy in most parts of the country. It is a charming shrub of bold, bushy habit, with prickly holly-like foliage, and scarlet and yellow, trumpet-shaped pendent flowers, borne in quantity. The shelter of a wall favours the growth and flowering of this handsome shrub, but it also succeeds well in the open if planted in rich, light soil, and in positions that are not exposed to cold and cutting winds.

Desmodium. See Lespedeza.

Deutzia (Saxifrageæ).

DEUTZIA CANDIDISSIMA.—This is a beautiful species with snowy-white flowers about half an inch in diameter. It was introduced in 1882.

D. CANESCENS.—Japan, 1837. This has slender branches, with ovate-lanceolate, roughish leaves, and terminal panicles of whitish flowers. There is a double-flowered variety.

D. CORYMBIFLORA.—A charming species with finely-toothed, ovate-lanceolate leaves and a rich abundance of white flowers. It grows freely and is a valuable addition to our flowering shrubs.

D. CORYMBOSA, from the Himalayas, has elliptic-lanceolate leaves and white flowers. It grows about 5 feet high.

D. CRENATA (*syn D. scabra* and *D. Fortunei*).—Japan, 1863. This is of stout, bushy growth, often reaching a height of 8 feet, and lateral spread of nearly as much. The ovate-lanceolate leaves are rough to the touch, and its slender but wiry stems are wreathed for a considerable distance along with racemes of pure-white flowers. It is a very distinct shrub, of noble port, and when in full flower is certainly one of the most ornamental of hardy shrubs. The double-flowered form, D. crenata flore-pleno, is one of the prettiest flowering shrubs in cultivation, the wealth of double flowers, not white as in the species, but tinged with reddish-purple, being highly attractive. D. crenata, Pride of Rochester, is another form with double-white flowers, and a most distinct and beautiful shrub. Two other very beautiful varieties are those known as D. crenata Watererii and D. crenata Wellsii.

D. DISCOLOR CARNEA and D. DISCOLOR LACTEA are the results of crossing D. scabra and D. discolor, the former having widely expanded and reflexed flowers which are of a blush colour, with the reverse of the petals of a deeper hue.

D. DISCOLOR PURPURASCENS (Yunnan, 1894) grows about a yard high and bears an abundance of flowers, which are tinted with rosy purple.

D. GRACILIS is a somewhat tender shrub of fully 18 inches high, with smooth leaves and pure-white flowers produced in the greatest freedom. It does well in warm, sheltered sites, but is most frequently seen as a greenhouse plant. A native of Japan.

D. KALMÆFLORA.—This is a hybrid form between D. parviflora and D. discolor purpurascens, and is a valuable flowering shrub and perfectly hardy. The flowers are rose-coloured with a deeper margin tint, and produced in large corymbs.

D. LEMOINEI has axillary racemes of very large white flowers. It is highly decorative, and is a hybrid between D. gracilis and D. parviflora.

D. STAMINEÆ.—Himalayas, 1841. This has white, sweet-scented flowers and oblong leaves, covered with a grey tomentum on the undersides.

The most suitable soil in which to cultivate the various Deutzias is rich, sandy loam, well drained.

Diervilla (Caprifoliaceæ).

DIERVILLA FLORIBUNDA (*syn D. multiflora* and *Weigelia floribunda*), from Japan, 1864, has narrow, tubular, purplish-coloured corollas, that are only slightly opened out at the mouth. The Diervillas are valuable decorative shrubs of free growth in good, rich loam, and bearing a great abundance of the showiest of flowers. For shrubbery planting they must ever rank high, the beautiful flowers and rich-green, ample leafage rendering them distinct and attractive.

D. GRANDIFLORA (*syn D. amabilis, D. arborea,* and *Weigelia amabilis*).—Japan. This is of larger growth than D. rosea, with strongly reticulated leaves, that are prominently veined on the underside, and much larger white flowers. It is a distinct and worthy species. There are some beautiful varieties of this species, named Isolinæ, Van Houttei, and Striata.

D. HORTENSIS (garden), from Japan, grows about 5 feet

in height, with ovate, stalked leaves and red or white flowers. D. hortensis nivea (1891) is a beautiful variety with pure-white flowers, which are produced abundantly.

D. ROSEA (*syn Weigelia rosea*).—China, 1844. This is a handsome hardy shrub of small stature, with ovate-lanceolate leaves, and clusters of showy pink, or sometimes white, flowers, that are produced in April and May. There are many good varieties of this shrub, of which the following are the most popular: D. rosea arborescens grandiflora; D. rosea Lavallii, with an abundance of crimson-red flowers; D. rosea Stelzneri, with an abundance of deep-red flowers; D. rosea candida, much like the latter, but bearing pure-white flowers; and D. rosea Looymansii aurea has beautiful golden leaves.

D. TRIFIDA (*syn D. canadensis*), North America, 1739, has ovate, serrated, glabrous leaves and yellow flowers.

Dimorphanthus. See Aralia.

Diospyros (Ebenaceæ).

DIOSPYROS KAKI COSTATA.—The Date Plum. China, 1789. Flowers whitish green. Fruit as big as a small apple; leaves leathery, entire, and broadly ovate; flowers and fruits in this country when afforded the protection of a wall. The fruit is superior to that of D. virginiana (Persimmon).

D. LOTUS, the common Date Plum, is a European species (1596), with purplish-white flowers, and oblong leaves that are reddish on the undersides. Both species want a light, warm soil, and sheltered situation.

D. VIRGINIANA.—The Persimmon, or Virginian Date Plum. North America, 1629. A small-growing tree, with coriaceous leaves, and greenish or golden-yellow flowers. In southern situations and by the seaside it is perfectly hardy, and succeeds well, but in other districts it is rather tender. The fruit is edible, yellow in colour, and about an inch in diameter.

Diplopappus. See Cassinia.

Dirca (Thymeleæ).

DIRCA PALUSTRIS.—Leather Wood. North America, 1750. A much-branched bush, of quite a tree-like character, but rarely more than 3 feet high. To the Daphnes it is nearly allied, and is close in resemblance; but there is a curious yellowish hue pervading the whole plant. The flowers are produced on the naked shoots in April, and are rendered conspicuous by reason of the pendent yellow stamens. They are borne in terminal clusters of three or four together. It delights to grow in a cool, moist soil, indeed it is only when so situated that the Leather Wood can be seen in a really thriving condition.

Discaria (Rhamneæ).

DISCARIA LONGISPINA.—This is at once a curious and beautiful shrub, of low, creeping growth, and poorly furnished with leaves, which, however, are amply made up for by the deep green of the shoots and stems, and which give to the plant almost the appearance of an evergreen. The flowers, which are bell-shaped and white, are almost lavishly produced, and as they last for a very long time, with only the pure white assuming a pinky tinge when subjected to excessive sunshine, the value of the shrub is still further enhanced. For planting against a mound of rock this scrambling shrub is of value, but the position should not be exposed to cold winds, for the plant is somewhat tender. From South America, and allied to the better known Colletias.

D. SERRATIFOLIA (*syn Colletia serratifolia*) is even a handsomer plant than the former, with minute serrated foliage, and sheets of small greenish-white, sweetly-scented flowers in June.

Drimys (Magnoliaceæ).

DRIMYS AROMATICA (*syn Tasmannia aromatica*).—Tasmanian Pepper Plant. Tasmania, 1843. This is, if we might say so, a more refined plant than D. Winteri, with smaller and narrower leaves, and smaller white or pink flowers. The plant, too, has altogether a faint reddish tinge, and is of upright growth. A native of Tasmania, and called by the natives the Pepper Plant, the fruit being used as a substitute for that condiment. Like the other species, the present plant is only hardy in warm, maritime places, and when afforded the protection of a wall.

D. WINTERI (*syn Wintera aromatica*).—Winter's Bark. South America, 1827. The fine evergreen character is the chief attraction of this American shrub, so far at least as garden ornamentation is concerned. With some persons even the greenish-white perfumed flowers are held in esteem, and it cannot be denied that a well-flowered plant has its own attractions. The long, narrow leaves are pale green above and glaucous beneath, and make the shrub of interest, both on account of their evergreen nature and brightness of tint. Unfortunately it is not very hardy, requiring even in Southern England a sunny wall to do it justice. They thrive in sandy loam, and bear pruning well.

Edwardsia. See Sophora.

Elæagnus (Elæagnaceæ).

Elæagnus argentea.—Silver Berry. North America, 1813. A spreading shrub 8 feet or 10 feet high, with lanceolate leaves clothed with silvery scales. The yellow, nodding flowers are axillary and clustered, and succeeded by pretty, silvery-ribbed berries.

E. glabra.—From Japan. This is one of the handsomest species, forming bushes of delightful green, leathery leaves, and with a neat and rather compact habit of growth. It grows with great freedom when planted in light, sandy soil, big globose bushes being the result of a few years' growth. Being perfectly hardy it is to be recommended if only for the ample leathery, deep-green foliage. The whitish flowers are inconspicuous. There is a form having the leaves margined with pale yellow, and known under the name of E. glabra variegata.

E. latifolia.—Himalayas, 1869. A deciduous, semi-climbing bush, with elliptic-lanceolate leaves that are often 5 inches long, and clustered, yellowish-white scented flowers. E. Simoni is a form of this.

E. longipes (*syn E. edulis*, *E. crispa*, and *E. multiflora*).—Japan, 1873. This species is also worthy of culture, whether for the ornamental flowers or fruit. It is a shrub 6 feet high, bearing an abundance of spotted, oval red berries on long footstalks. Quite hardy.

E. macrophylla.—Japan. This is of robust growth, with handsome, dark-green leaves, purplish branch tips, and greenish-yellow flowers in autumn. The leaves are thick of texture, often fully 3 inches long, glossy-green above and silvery beneath. The latter is all the more remarkable, as the leaves have the habit of curling up their edges, and thus revealing the light, silvery tint of the undersides. It thrives well in light, sandy peat, and may be relied upon as one of the hardiest of shrubs.

E. ROTUNDIFOLIA (*syn E. multiflora*).—An interesting and perfectly hardy species, growing about 5 feet high, and remarkable for the great wealth of pretty scarlet and amber-coloured berries. The flowers are not very showy, but this is made up by the beautiful silvery leaves, most pronounced on the undersides, and wealth of fruit, which hangs on long stalks like cherries.

Other species of less interest are E. pungens (*syn E. reflexa*), of which there is a variegated variety; and E. umbellata, of good habit and with large leaves and clustered white, fragrant flowers. The various species and varieties of Elæagnus may all be cultivated in light, free soil, and from experiments that were recently made, they have been found of great value for planting by the seaside. They are popularly known as the Wild Olives and Evergreen Oleasters, and are capable of withstanding long periods of drought.

Embothrium (Proteaceæ).

EMBOTHRIUM COCCINEUM.—Fire Bush. South America, 1851. This is a beautiful shrub, of tall growth, with flowers of great interest and beauty. Except in warm and favoured situations, it is not very hardy, and should always be grown as a wall plant. The fiery scarlet, orange-tinted flowers, resembling somewhat those of the Honeysuckle, are very beautiful by the first weeks of May. It grows to about 6 feet in height in Southern England, and is, when in full flower, a shrub of unusual beauty. Sandy peat.

Empetrum (Empetraceæ).

EMPETRUM NIGRUM and its variety E. nigrum rubrum are of low, heath-like growth, the former with pinky and the latter with brownish flowers. The species is a native of Britain, while the variety hails from Chili, from whence it was introduced in 1833. Damp, peaty soil.

Enkianthus (Ericaceæ).

ENKIANTHUS CAMPANULATUS.—Japan. This is the commonest species in cultivation, with elliptic and sharply-toothed leaves, and clusters of drooping, greenish-white flowers, which are, in some cases, freely produced, and particularly when the shrub is planted in rather dampish, light, peaty soil. There is a white-flowered species, also of Japanese origin, named E. japonicus, and another with red flowers called E. Himalaicus. E. cernuus, recently introduced from Japan, has reddish drooping flowers.

Ephedra (Gnetaceæ).

EPHEDRA NEBRODENSIS (*syn E. distachya*), South-West Europe, 1750, bears whitish flowers, which are succeeded by scarlet berries.

E. VULGARIS (*syn Ephedra monostachya*), from Siberia, 1772, is a half-hardy shrub of trailing habit, with inconspicuous whitish flowers. The fact of its thriving in very poor soil, or on rocky situations, is the only reason why it is introduced here.

Epigæa (Ericaceæ).

EPIGÆA REPENS.—Ground Laurel, or New England Mayflower. Northern United States, 1736. This is, perhaps, in so far as stature is concerned, hardly worthy of a place in our list, yet it is such a pretty and useful shrub, though rarely rising more than 6 inches from the ground, that we cannot well pass it over. For planting beneath Pine or other trees, where it can spread about at will, this prostrate shrub is most at home. There it enlivens the spot with its pretty evergreen foliage, and sweet-scented, white or pinky flowers. It is quite hardy, and should be planted in peaty soil in the shade.

Ercilla (Phytolaccaceæ).

ERCILLA SPICATA (*syn Bridgesia spicata*).—Chili, 1840. A small-growing, half-climbing shrub, with leathery, deep-green leaves and inconspicuous purplish flowers. Hailing from Chili, it is not very hardy, but given the protection of a wall, or planted against a tree-stump, it soon forms a neat mass of evergreen foliage. It is excellent for planting in dry soils.

Erica (Ericaceæ).

ERICA CARNEA.—South Europe, 1763. This is one of the most beautiful and desirable of hardy Heaths, on account of the richly-coloured flowers and early season at which they are produced. In the typical species the flowers are pink or flesh-coloured, and produced in January and February. It is a dwarf, compact growing species, with bright-green foliage. There is a form with pure-white flowers, named E. carnea alba, or E. herbacea, but although distinct and beautiful, it is not of so robust growth as the parent.

E. CILIARIS.—A pretty native species, with ciliate glandular leaves, and racemes of highly-coloured, rosy flowers. Found in Dorsetshire and Cornwall.

E. CINEREA.—Grey-leaved Heath. In this species, also a native of Britain, the flowers are of a reddish-purple colour, and borne in dense terminal racemes. There are numerous varieties, including a white-flowered E. cinerea alba; E. cinerea atro-purpurea, bearing dark-purple flowers; E. cinerea atro-sanguinea, dark-red flowers; E. cinerea coccinea, scarlet; E. cinerea purpurea, purple flowers; and E. cinerea rosea, with deep rose-coloured flowers.

E. CODONODES (South Europe) is a beautiful species of from 6 to 10 feet in height, and gracefully irregular habit of growth. The charming pinky-white flowers are very freely produced, and are of particular value as appearing so early in the season from January to April. In sandy peat it succeeds well, and is hardy in many parts of the country.

E. MEDITERRANEA.—Mediterranean Heath. Portugal, 1648. This is a robust-growing species, of rather erect habit, and often attaining to fully a yard in height. Flowers abundantly produced, and of a pretty pinky hue. Of this there are several varieties, the following being best known: E. mediterranea hibernica, found in Ireland; E. mediterranea alba, with white flowers; E. mediterranea nana, of very dwarf growth; and E. mediterranea rubra, with showy, deep-red flowers.

E. SCOPARIA and E. ERECTA are desirable species, the former bearing greenish flowers, and the latter of decidedly upright growth.

E. TETRALIX.—Cross-leaved Heath. A native species of low and bushy growth, with close umbels or terminal clusters of pretty pinky flowers. The varieties of this most worthy of notice are E. Tetralix alba, white flowered; E. Tetralix Mackiana, crimson flowered; E. Tetralix rubra, deep-red flowers; and E. Tetralix bicolor, with particoloured flowers.

E. VAGANS.—Cornish Heath. A native species, bearing pinky-white flowers, but there are forms with white and red flowers, named E. vagans alba and E. vagans rubra.

The various kinds of Heath succeed best either in peaty soil, or that composed for the greater part of light, sandy loam, but many will grow and flower freely if planted in rich yellow loam. They are very desirable plants, either for bed formation, for rockwork ornamentation, or for planting around the shrubbery margins. Propagation is effected either by cuttings or subdivisions, but seedlings of several species spring up freely under favourable conditions.

Eriobotrya. See Photinia.

Escallonia (Saxifrageæ).

ESCALLONIA EXONIENSIS (1891) is a pretty, hardy shrub, with small, deep-green, ovate leaves and a rich profusion of pink and white pendent flowers. It is said to be of hybrid origin.

E. FLORIBUNDA (*syn E. montevidensis*).—New Grenada, 1827. This is one of the handsomest species, bearing long, arching clusters of white flowers. It is a very desirable shrub for wall or lattice-work covering, against which it grows rapidly, and soon forms an object of great beauty by reason of its neat foliage and graceful habit, as also wealth of pretty flowers.

E. ILLINATA.—Chili, 1830. This should also be included, it being a handsome and pretty-flowered plant.

E. LANGLEYENSIS is a hybrid between E. macrantha and E. Philippiana. It is a beautiful form, though not perfectly hardy, with rosy-purple flowers which are produced freely.

E. MACRANTHA.—Chiloe, 1848. This is a general favourite in English gardens, where it succeeds well, but especially in maritime parts of the country. It is of stout growth, 6 feet or more in height, of spreading habit, and with elliptical, serrulated, bright-green leaves, and clusters of crimson-red flowers produced in summer. For wall-covering this is an almost invaluable shrub, although it succeeds well as a standard in all but the colder parts of the country. Any free, open soil suits it well, but thorough drainage must be attended to. There are several very distinct and good varieties, such as E. macrantha sanguinea, with flowers deeper in colour than those of the parent plant; and E. macrantha Ingrami, a profuse-blooming and very desirable form.

E. Philippiana.—Valdivia, 1873. When seen as a standard bush, and loaded with its myriads of tiny white flowers, this must rank amongst the handsomest members of the family. It is very hardy, and retains its foliage throughout the winter. The hybrid form, E. leucantha, deserves recognition, for even as late as November the small spikes of pretty white flowers, which contrast nicely with the neat, evergreen foliage, are produced abundantly.

E. pterocladon.—Patagonia, 1854. This is remarkable for the curiously-winged branches, which give to the shrub a rather peculiar and distinct appearance. The freely-produced flowers are white or pink.

E. rubra.—Chili, 1827. This has less handsome leaves and flowers than the above, but it is, all the same, a beautiful plant. The flowers vary a good deal in depth of colouring, and may be seen of all tints between pure white and red.

The Escallonias are all of very free growth in any light, warm, sandy, and well-drained soil, and are readily propagated, especially in maritime situations.

Eucryphia (Rosaceæ).

Eucryphia cordifolia (Chili, 1851) has heart-shaped leaves and large white flowers; while E. cordifolia Cavanilles (Chili,1897) has dark, persistent foliage, blunter and more rounded than those of the species, and beautiful white flowers. Against a wall it has attained to 10 feet in height in the South of Ireland.

E. pinnatifolia.—Chili, 1880. This shrub is as yet rare in cultivation, and is not suited for the colder or more exposed parts of the country. It is, however, a singularly distinct and beautiful shrub, with deep glossy-green, pinnate foliage, and bearing large, pure-white flowers often 3 inches across that are rendered all the more conspicuous by the golden-yellow anthers. As an ornamental shrub it is well worthy of cultivation. In so far as its hardihood in this climate is concerned, it may be mentioned that in various parts of England and Ireland it has stood in the open ground unharmed for several years back. Light, sandy, well-drained peat and a sunny situation would seem to meet with its requirements.

Eugenia. See Myrtus.

Euonymus (Celastrineæ).

EUONYMUS AMERICANUS.—American Spindle Tree. North America, 1686. This is a deciduous or semi-evergreen shrub, of about 6 feet in height, found over a wide area in Canada and the United States. It is of partially erect growth, with long and lithe branches, covered with pleasing light-green bark. The greenish-purple flowers appear in June, and are succeeded by rough, warted, brilliant-scarlet capsules, which are particularly showy and attractive. It likes a shady situation, and rich, rather damp soil.

E. EUROPÆUS.—West Asia, Europe (Britain), etc. An indigenous species, rarely exceeding 6 feet in height, with greenish white, fœtid flowers. This shrub is rendered very effective in autumn by reason of the pale-scarlet fruit, which, when fully ripe, and having split open, reveals the orange-coloured arils of the seeds. It, too, delights to grow in the shade.

E. FIMBRIATUS, Japan and India, and its handsome variegated form, E. fimbriatus foliis variegatus et argenteo maculatus, are rather too tender for cultivation in this country, even in southern districts, and where afforded wall protection. E. verrucosus and E. atropurpureus are also worthy of cultivation.

E. LATIFOLIUS.—Broad-leaved Spindle Tree. A European species (1730), deciduous, and growing from 10 feet to sometimes fully 20 feet in height. The leaves are bright, shining green, and much larger than those of our native species. Flowers, purplish-white, appearing in June; the capsules large, deep red, and when open contrasting very effectively with the bright orange arils in which the seeds are enveloped. It is a very distinct and beautiful, small-growing lawn tree, and succeeding, as it does, best in shade is an extra qualification.

E. NANUS (Caucasus, 1830) is a small-growing rockery shrub, with deep-green lanceolate, entire leaves, and greenish-white flowers in July. It is a neat under shrub.

Eurybia. See Olearia.

Exochorda (Rosaceæ).

EXOCHORDA GRANDIFLORA (*syn Spiræa grandiflora*).—North China. This handsome shrub forms a much branched, spreading bush about 4 feet to 6 feet high, and flowers abundantly in May. The habit is similar to that of a shrubby Spiræa, but the pure-white flowers are as large as those of some of the species of Cherry, and quite unlike those of any known species of Spiræa. The flowers are liable to injury sometimes from late spring frosts, but the plant itself is quite hardy. As a bush on the lawn it is nevertheless highly ornamental and desirable.

Fabiana (Solanaceæ).

FABIANA IMBRICATA.—Chili, 1838. This is, unfortunately, not hardy in any but the milder maritime parts of

England and Ireland. It is a charming shrub of Heather-like appearance, with small, crowded leaves, and pure-white flowers produced abundantly in May. Planted at the base of a southern wall it does best, and where it thrives it is certainly one of our handsomest half-hardy shrubs. Light, loamy soil will suit it.

Fatsia (Araliaceæ).

FATSIA JAPONICA (*syns Aralia japonica* and *A. Sieboldii*).—Japan, 1858. This is of no particular value as a flowering shrub, but being hardy in most districts, and having large handsome leaves that impart to it a tropical appearance, it is well worthy of culture. The flowers are ivory-white and produced in large umbels towards the end of autumn, but our early frosts too often mar their beauty. In this country it grows about 10 feet high, and is usually what is termed "leggy" in appearance, and thrives well in any good loamy soil if fairly dry. There are two varieties, aurea and variegata.

Fendlera (Saxifrageæ).

FENDLERA RUPICOLA.—Mexico, 1888. A low-growing shrub, peculiar to the dry, rocky parts of the United States, particularly the south-western district. It grows about a yard high, and bears a great profusion of white or bluish-white flowers, that are rendered very conspicuous by reason of the bright-yellow stamens. It is the only known species, and is nearly allied to the Saxifrages. Any fairly good garden soil will suit it well, but it wants to be planted where superfluous moisture is quickly carried off.

Flacourtia. See Idesia.

Forsythia (Oleaceæ).

FORSYTHIA SUSPENSA (*syn F. Fortunei* and *F. Sieboldii*).—Japan and China, 1864. A slender-growing shrub, with variable leaves, and long, trailing shoots. The flowers are abundantly produced, are of a beautiful golden tint, and bell-shaped, and, being of good substance, last for a long time. Either as a wall plant, or for using in some sheltered corner, and where the branches can spread about at will, it forms a very distinct and handsome shrub, and one that is perfectly hardy and quite indifferent as regards the quality of soil in which it is planted. There are several forms of this pretty shrub, but as they do not differ to any great extent from the species, are hardly worthy of consideration.

F. SUSPENSA INTERMEDIA, with bright golden flowers, is a garden hybrid (1891) between F. suspensa and F. viridissima.

F. VIRIDISSIMA.—Japan, 1845. This is another desirable species, but it is not comparable in point of beauty with the former. It is usually of strong, erect growth, with stout shoots, wreathed with bright-yellow flowers towards the end of winter. It is a very beautiful shrub, and a valuable addition to the winter or early spring flowering section.

Fothergilla (Hamamelideæ).

FOTHERGILLA ALNIFOLIA (*syn F. Gardeni*). — North-Eastern America, 1765. This is an ungainly habited shrub, of dwarf growth, the branches being somewhat slender and crooked. The flowers are white, sweetly scented, and produced in dense terminal spikes. It is perfectly hardy, and succeeds best in sandy peat.

Fraxinus (Oleaceæ).

FRAXINUS MARIESII.—Northern China, 1880. This is hardy in most parts of the country. The whole tree is quite glabrous except the petioles, which are clothed with a dense pubescence. Flowers pure white, and arranged in large dense panicles.

F. ORNUS (*syn F. argentea, F. rotundifolia*, and *Ornus europœa*).—Manna Ash. South Europe, 1730. This is a handsome tree, especially when young and vigorous, and by far the most ornamental species in cultivation. For planting in situations where large-growing subjects would be out of place this is a valuable tree, while the wealth of flowers renders it particularly interesting and effective. It rarely exceeds 30 feet in height, with leaves not unlike those of the common Ash, and conspicuous panicles of light, feathery, white petaliferous flowers, produced usually in great abundance all over the tree. Perfectly hardy.

F. ORNUS SEROTINA ALBA and F. ORNUS SEROTINA VIOLACEA are beautiful seedling forms that were raised in France, and on account of their dwarf habit and profusion of flowers are well worthy of attention. The flowers of the first-named variety are pure white, the stamens having at first yellow anthers, which speedily turn to a rich blackish-brown. The other differs but little, only in the flowers, which are of a distinct greyish-violet hue, while the leaves are of a darker shade of green, and the leaflets longer and narrower.

F. XANTHOXYLOIDES.—Himalayas, 1845. A small-growing tree with three to five pairs of leaflets, and dense heads of brownish flowers which appear before the leaves. These are the only species that can be considered as ornamental flowering. They all succeed in rich, dampish, well-drained loam.

Fremontia (Malvaceæ).

FREMONTIA CALIFORNICA.—California, 1851. A handsome, deciduous Californian shrub, that is scarcely hardy enough for the open air without protection. In Southern England and Ireland, however, it does well, and all the better if planted within the influence of the sea. The large bright-yellow flowers are often about 2 inches across, and produced singly along the branches, while the leaves are large, lobed, and of an enticing shade of green. Planted against a wall, in good, dampish loam, it succeeds well.

Fuchsia (Onagraceæ).

FUCHSIA MACROSTEMMA GLOBOSA (*syn F. globosa*).—Chili. This is readily recognized by the globose form assumed by the incurved sepals, while the purplish-violet flowers are smaller and less showy than those of F. Riccartoni. Hardihood about similar to the following.

F. RICCARTONI.—This seedling from F. m. globosa is one of the two hardiest varieties, but, except in warm, maritime districts, it is by no means satisfactory. Where it does well it is a shrub of great beauty, and blooms profusely. This Fuchsia has red, straight sepals, and a purple corolla. In favoured districts it may frequently be seen as much as 12 feet high, and is then during the flowering period an object of great beauty. It originated at Riccarton, near Edinburgh, about 1830.

Garrya (Cornaceæ).

GARRYA ELLIPTICA.—California, 1818. This is a handsome shrub, with dark-green coriaceous leaves, resembling very nearly those of the Evergreen Oak. The long, tesselated catkins, of a peculiar yellowish-green colour, render the plant one of much interest and beauty. As a wall plant it thrives well, the slight protection thus afforded favouring the growth and expansion of the catkins. For planting in the shrubbery it is also well suited, where it oft-times attains to a height of 6 feet, and is bushy in proportion. It is well to bear in mind that there are male and female plants of the Garrya, and that the former is the more ornamental. Good rich, well-drained loam will suit this shrub well. Pruning should take place immediately after flowering.

G. Fremonti (North-West America) resembles the former, but the catkins are shorter and less pendulous, while G. macrophylla (Mexico, 1846) rarely exceeds 6 feet in height, with short racemes.

Gaultheria (Ericaceæ).

Gaultheria nummularioides (*syn G. nummulariæ* and *G. repens*).—Himalayas, 1884. This is a neat Alpine species, with small and very dark-green leaves and Lily-of-the-Valley-like flowers that are tinged with pink. It likes a shady situation and vegetable soil. For planting on the rockwork, amongst tree roots, or beneath the shade of trees, the Gaultherias are particularly suitable. Light, but rich vegetable soil suits them best.

G. procumbens.—Canada Tea, or Creeping Wintergreen. North America, 1762. This is of much smaller growth than the following, rarely rising to a greater height than about half a foot, with lanceolate, serrated leaves, and pendulous axillary clusters of white flowers.

G. Shallon.—North-West America, 1826. Growing in favourable situations to fully a yard in height, this distinct evergreen shrub, which is fairly common in cultivation, is particularly valuable, as it thrives well under the shade and drip of trees. It is a rambling plant, with ovate-cordate, almost sessile leaves, and bears tiny white flowers tinged with red that are succeeded by purplish edible fruit. G. Shallon acutifolia has more sharply-pointed leaves than those of the species.

G. TRICOPHYLLA (Himalayas and China) is a dwarf, tufted, evergreen species, with pinky-white flowers which are as long as the leaves.

Genista (Leguminosæ). See Spartium.

GENISTA ANGLICA (Britain).—This grows to about a couple of feet in height, is smooth throughout, and bears terminal, few-flowered racemes.

G. ÆTNENSIS (*syn Spartium ætnensis*).—Etna Broom. Sicily and Sardinia, 1816. This is a large-growing species of elegant growth, and remarkable for the abundance of yellow flowers with which it is literally covered in August. Than this South-European Pea-flower, perhaps not another member of the family is more worthy of culture, the neat, elegant habit of growth and profusion of flowers rendering it a plant of particular interest and beauty. It is quite hardy, thrives in any light soil if well drained, and is readily propagated from seed, which it ripens in abundance.

G. ANXANTICA.—Naples, 1818. This is a nearly allied species to our native G. tinctoria, and is of dwarf growth with a rich abundance of golden-yellow flowers that are produced towards the end of summer.

G. CINEREA (*syn G. ramosissima*), from South Europe, is a very beautiful and desirable species, a yard high, with striated branches, and bearing in July slender twigs of the brightest yellow flowers.

G. EPHEDROIDES.—Corsica and Sardinia, 1832. With small and abundantly-produced flowers, this resembles Ephedra, hence its name.

G. GERMANICA.—Germany, 1773. This is a handsome

rock-garden shrub, of fully 18 inches in height, with arching stems and a plentiful supply of bright flowers during the summer and autumn months.

G. HISPANICA.—South-Western Europe, 1759. This species resembles our common Broom, but the branches are not angular. The large, yellow, fragrant flowers appear in July. There is a charming double-flowered variety named G. hispanica flore-pleno.

G. LUSITANICA.—Portugal, 1771. This is remarkable for its opposite branches, is of spiny growth, and one of the earliest to appear in flower.

G. MONOSPERMA.—South Europe, 1690. This has white flowers, and is of value as a seaside shrub, and grows well in almost pure sand. A native of the Mediterranean coast.

G. PILOSA.—Greenweed. Europe (Britain). This is a dense, prostrate native species, with bright-yellow blossoms produced freely during May and June. A delightful rock shrub, and one that will succeed well almost in pure gravel.

G. PROSTRATA.—Burgundy and Alps of Jura, 1775. A small-growing species suitable for rock gardening, and of spreading bushy growth. Flowers small, but ornamental, and produced in May and June.

G. RADIATA (*syn Spartium radiatum*).—South Europe, 1758. This is a slender-growing shrub, about 18 inches high, with narrow leaflets, and terminal heads of yellow flowers produced in summer.

G. SAGITTALIS.—South Europe, 1750. With its peculiarly winged and jointed stems, which are of a deep-green colour, this is one of the most distinct forms. The flowers are few but pretty, and with the dwarf habit render the plant an excellent subject for rockwork.

G. TINCTORIA.—Dyers' Greenweed. Europe (Britain), North and West Asia. This is a spineless species, and bears a profusion of yellow flowers from July onwards.

The double-flowering variety, G. tinctoria flore-pleno, is, in so far as ornamental qualities are concerned, superior to the parent form.

G. TINCTORIA ELATIOR (*syn G. elatior*) grows to 12 feet in height, is of free, spreading growth, and a very handsome plant. The flowers, which are individually small and yellow, are so thickly produced that the shrub, in late summer, has the appearance of a sheet of gold.

G. TRIANGULARIS (*syn G. triquetra*).—South Europe, 1815. This is a decidedly good garden plant, and of neat, trailing habit. The stems are three-sided, and the flowers golden-yellow and plentifully produced. A native of South Europe, and perfectly hardy in almost any position.

The above include most of the hardy Genistas, though G. capitata and G. daurica, both very ornamental kinds, might be added to the list. They are all very hardy, free-flowering shrubs, of simple culture, and succeed well in any light and rather dry soil.

Gleditschia (Leguminosæ).

GLEDITSCHIA TRIACANTHOS.—Honey Locust. United States, 1700. As an ornamental hardy tree this is well worthy the attention of planters, the pinnate and bipinnate foliage being particularly elegant, while the greenish flowers, though individually small, are borne in such quantities of fascicled racemes as to attract notice. The stem and branches are armed with formidable prickles, but there is a form in which the prickles are absent. A native of North America, and readily cultivated in any soil of even fair quality. For town planting it is a valuable tree. There is a good weeping variety named G. triacanthos pendula. G. SINENSIS (*syn G. horrida*).—China, 1774. This nearly resembles the latter, and is occasionally to be met with in cultivation in this country; while G. MONOSPERMA (United States, 1723), with greenish flowers, is not particularly attractive.

Glycine. See Wistaria.

Gordonia (Ternstræmiaceæ).

GORDONIA LASIANTHUS.—Loblolly Bay. North America, 1739. A shrub of great beauty, but one that, unfortunately, is rarely to be seen outside the walls of a botanic garden. It is of Camellia-like growth, with large, white, sweetly-fragrant flowers about 3 inches across, produced during July and August.

G. PUBESCENS.—North America, 1774. This is of smaller growth than the latter, rarely exceeding about 6 feet in height, with large white fragrant flowers that are rendered all the more conspicuous by the tufts of golden stamens. Both species are somewhat tender, although hailing from the coast, swampy grounds of the southern States of North America. Planted in favoured sites, they usually grow freely in light, peaty soil, or that containing a large admixture of decayed leaf soil.

Grabowskia (Solanaceæ).

GRABOWSKIA BŒRHAAVIÆFOLIA.—Peru, 1780. This is occasionally to be seen in sheltered and favoured gardens, but it is not to be relied upon in other than southern and seaside districts. The plant is of no particular interest to the cultivator, the outline being ungainly, while the pale-blue flowers are both dull and uninteresting. It belongs to the Solanum family, and is only worth cultivating as a curiosity. Light, warm soil and a sunny position are necessities in the cultivation of this shrub.

Griselinia (Cornaceæ).

GRISELINIA LITTORALIS.—New Zealand, 1872. This forms a compact bush of moderate size, and is fairly hardy. The leaves are of a light, pleasing green shade, coriaceous, and glossy, and remain on the plant during winter, while the flowers are minute and uninteresting. It is an excellent shrub for the seaside, and, moreover, will succeed well in stiff soils where many other plants would refuse to grow.

G. LUCIDA, from New Zealand, with obliquely ovate leaves and small flowers, is less hardy than the preceding.

Gymnocladus (Leguminosæ).

GYMNOCLADUS CANADENSIS. — Kentucky Coffee Tree. Canada, 1748. When in full leafage this is a distinct and beautiful tree, the foliage hanging in well-rounded masses, and presenting a pretty effect by reason of the loose and tufted appearance of the masses of finely-divided leaves. Leaves often 3 feet long, bipinnate, and composed of numerous bluish-green leaflets. Flowers white, borne in loose spikes in the beginning of summer, and succeeded by flat, somewhat curved brown pods. It prefers a rich, strong soil or alluvial deposit.

G. CHINENSIS.—Soap Tree. China, 1889. Readily distinguished from the American species by its much smaller and more numerous leaflets, smaller flowers, and thicker fruit pod. It is not very hardy in this country unless in the milder seaside districts. The fruit is used by the Chinese women to wash their hair, hence the popular name of Soap Tree.

Halesia (Styracaceæ).

HALESIA DIPTERA (*syn H. reticulata*).—North America, 1758. This is not so suitable for our climate as H. tetraptera, though in southern parts of the country it forms a neat, healthy bush, the white flowers being produced freely. It is distinguished, as the name indicates, by having two wings to the seed vessel, H. tetraptera having four.

H. HISPIDA (*syn Pterostyrax hispidum*).—Japan, 1875. This is a shrub of perfect hardihood, free growth, and very floriferous. The flowers, which are pure white, and in long racemes, greatly resemble those of the Snowdrop Tree. Leaves broad and slightly dentated. It is a handsome shrub, of free growth, in light, sandy loam, and quite hardy even when fully exposed.

H. PARVIFLORA (Florida, 1802) has smaller white, drooping flowers than those of our commonly cultivated plant.

H. TETRAPTERA.—Snowdrop Tree. North America, 1756. This is a very ornamental tall-growing shrub, of somewhat loose growth, and bearing flowers which resemble, both in size and appearance, those of our common Snowdrop. It is one of the most ornamental of all the small-growing American trees, and richly deserves a place in every collection, on account of the profusion with which the flowers are produced in April and May. They are snow-white, drooping, and produced in lateral fascicles of eight or ten together. It is a native of river banks in North Carolina, and is well suited for cultivation in this country. Light, peaty soil will grow it to perfection.

H. TETRAPTERA MECHANI (1892) is a seedling variety with smaller and shorter stalked flowers and thicker, rugose leaves.

Halimodendron (Leguminosæ).

HALIMODENDRON ARGENTEUM (*syn Robinia Halimodendron*). —Salt tree. A native of Asiatic Russia (1779), having silvery foliage, and pink or purplish-pink flowers, axillary or fascicled. It is a neat and pretty shrub, that is rendered valuable as succeeding well in maritime districts. Quite hardy and of free growth in sandy soil.

H. ARGENTEUM FLORE-PURPUREUM (1894) has deep rosy-purple flowers.

Hamamelis (Hamamelideæ).

HAMAMELIS JAPONICA.—The Japanese Witch Hazel. Japan, 1862. This is a small species with lemon-yellow flowers. H. japonica arborea is a taller growing variety, with primrose-yellow petals, and a deep claret calyx. The flowers are borne in clusters in early spring. Rarely in this country do we find this species of greater height than about 8 feet, but it is of bushy growth, though somewhat straggling in appearance. As early as the beginning of January this Witch Hazel may be found in bloom, the bare branches being studded here and there with the curious-shaped flowers, these having bright-yellow, twisted petals and reddish calyces. H. j. Zuccariniana is a very desirable free-flowering variety, with pale-yellow petals and a greenish-brown calyx.

H. MOLLIS.—China, 1898. This is a distinct species with large leaves, often 5 inches long, which are thickly covered on the undersides with a felt-like down. The flowers are pale yellow, and produced early in the year.

H. VIRGINIANA.—Virginian Witch Hazel. North America, 1736. This has smaller flowers than H. j. arborea, and they are plentifully produced in autumn or early winter. In this country it assumes the shape of an open bush of about 6 feet in height, but is usually of untidy appearance from the branches being irregularly disposed.

They all delight in cool, rather moist soil, and are of value for their early-flowering nature.

Hedysarum (Leguminosæ).

HEDYSARUM MULTIJUGUM.—South Mongolia, 1883. Hardly twenty years have elapsed since this pretty shrub was introduced into England, and it is at present rather rare in our gardens. It is a decided acquisition, if only for the production of flowers at a time when these are scarce. Usually the flowering time is in August, but frequently in the first weeks of October the pretty flowers are still full of beauty. It is of bushy habit, from 4 feet to 5 feet high, with oblong leaflets, in number from twenty to thirty-five, which are pea-green above and downy on the undersides. Flowers bright red, and produced in axillary racemes, and longer than the leaves. It is perfectly hardy, and grows freely in porous decomposed leaf-soil.

H. MICROCALYX (Himalayas, 1877) is a sub-shrub with violet-red flowers.

Heimia. See Nesæa.

Helianthemum (Cistineæ).

HELIANTHEMUM ATRIPICIFOLIUM.—Spain, 1569. The branches of this species are white from tomentum, with broadly-ovate stalked leaves and large yellow flowers.

H. HALIMIFOLIUM.—Spain, 1656. This species is of erect habit, 3 feet or 4 feet high, and with leaves reminding one of those of the Sea Purslane. It is an evergreen, and has large bright-yellow flowers, slightly spotted at the base of the petals.

H. LÆVIPES (*syn Cistus lœvipes*).—South-Western Europe. A dwarf shrub, with Heath-like leaves, and yellow flowers that are produced in great abundance.

H. LASIANTHUM (*syns H. formosum* and *Cistus formosus*).—Spain and Portugal, 1780. This is a beautiful species, but not hardy unless in the South and West. It has large, bright-yellow flowers, with a deep reddish-purple blotch at the base of each petal.

H. LAVENDULÆFOLIUM has Lavender-like leaves, with the under surface hoary, and yellow flowers. A native of the Mediterranean regions, and introduced in 1817.

H. LIBONATES.—This species bears dark-green Rosemary-like leaves, and yellow flowers that are produced very abundantly. South Europe.

H. PILOSUM.—South of France, 1831. This bears white flowers that are of good substance, and about an inch across.

H. POLIFOLIUM (*syn H. pulverulentum*).—Europe (Britain) and North Africa. This is a neat-growing shrub, of very dwarf growth, with hairy leaves and yellow flowers; and H. polifolium roseum has pretty rosy-red flowers.

H. UMBELLATUM.—South Europe, 1731. A neat, small-growing species, with white flowers and glossy-green leaves covered with a rusty-white tomentum beneath.

H. VULGARE.—Common Rock Rose. Europe (Britain), North Africa, and West Asia. A widely-distributed native plant, of dwarf growth, with linear-oblong, hairy leaves, and usually yellow flowers. H. vulgare nummularium differs in having the leaves green and sub-orbicular, with yellow flowers. H. vulgare barbatum is of erect habit, with silky, hairy, oval leaves. H. vulgare mutabile bears pale-rose flowers, marked with yellow at the base. H. vulgare grandiflorum is remarkable for the large, bright-yellow flowers, and is one of the most beautiful and worthy varieties. H. vulgare ovalifolium (*syn H. serpyllifolium*) bears yellow flowers and ovate leaves, with the margins revolute. H. vulgare hyssopifolium bears reddish flowers, but the colouring varies considerably, and saffron is not uncommon.

The Rockroses are very valuable shrubs, in that they will succeed on poor, gravelly banks where few other plants could eke out an existence. They cannot withstand stiff soil, nor that at all inclined to be damp, their favourite resorts being exposed, rocky ground, and dry, gravelly banks. Being readily increased from cuttings, which take root well under a hand glass or in a cool house, it is advisable, at least with the more tender forms, to have at hand a stock, so that blanks in the shrubbery may be filled up.

Hibiscus (Malvaceæ).

Hibiscus syriacus (*syn Althæa frutex*).—Syrian Mallow. Syria, 1596. An old occupant of our gardens, and one that cannot be too freely cultivated. When favourably situated, it often reaches 6 feet in height, with three-lobed, neatly-toothed leaves, and large, showy blossoms that are borne towards the end of summer. The typical species has purplish flowers, with a crimson spot at the base of each petal, but others, varying in colour from snow-white to purple and blue, are common in cultivation. H. syriacus cœlestis bears bright-blue flowers, while H. syriacus variegatus has beautifully variegated foliage. Of the double-flowered forms, there are several beautiful and worthy plants, the following list containing some of the best varieties of this popular shrub :—

H. syriacus albo-pleno.
,, amaranthus.
,, amplissima.
,, ardens.
,, cærulea.
,, carnea plena.
,, De la Veuve.
,, elegantissimum.
,, fastuosa.
,, Lady Stanley.
,, Leopoldii.

H. syriacus lilacina plena.
,, painted lady.
,, pæoniæflora.
,, puniceus plenus.
,, rosea plena.
,, rubra plena.
,, spectabilis plena.
,, totus albus.
,, violacea.
,, violet clare.

Hippophæ (Elæagnaceæ).

Hippophæ rhamnoides.—Sea Buckthorn, or Sallow Thorn. Though generally considered as a seaside shrub, the Sea Buckthorn is by no means exclusively so, thriving well, and attaining to large dimensions, in many inland situations. The yellow diœcious flowers are not at all conspicuous, but this is amply compensated for by the beautiful silvery-like leaves and wealth of fruit borne by the shrub. In not a few instances, for fully a foot in length, the branches are smothered with crowded clusters of bright orange berries, which render the shrub during November and December both distinct and effective. It does best in sandy soil, and is readily increased from suckers, which are usually plentifully produced by old plants. For sea-side planting it is one of our most valuable shrubs, succeeding, as it does, well down even to high-water mark, and where the foliage is lashed with the salt spray.

H. SALICIFOLIA, from the Himalayas, is a nearly allied form.

Holbœllia (Berberideæ).

HOLBŒLLIA LATIFOLIA (*syn Stauntonia latifolia*).—Himalayas, 1840. An evergreen climbing shrub that is more often found under glass than out of doors. In the South of England, however, it is quite hardy against a sunny wall. It grows 12 feet high, with shining green leathery leaves, and fragrant purplish-green flowers. H. latifolia angustifolia has decidedly narrower leaves than the species, but is in no other way different.

Hortensia. See Hydrangea.

Hydrangea (Saxifrageæ).

HYDRANGEA ARBORESCENS.—North America, 1736. This is a plant of large growth, but the flowers are greenish-white, and by no means conspicuous. H. arborescens grandiflora is a new variety of American origin, and valuable for the pure-white flowers, which are often 10 inches across, and produced in succession from June till frost sets in. In general appearance it resembles our Snowball tree, the flowers being sterile.

H. HORTENSIS (*syn Hortensia opuloides*).—China, 1790.

This is an old-fashioned garden shrub that is only hardy in the south and west of these islands and in the vicinity of the sea. In some of the forms nearly all the flowers are sterile, the calyx-lobes being greatly expanded, and in others the outer flowers only are sterile. According to the nature of the soil the flowers vary much in colour, some being pure white, others pink, and others of varying shades of blue. There are some very beautiful and distinct varieties, such as H. hortensis japonica; H. hortensis Otaksa, with large panicles of sterile blue flowers; H. hortensis rosea-alba, with large rosy flowers; H. hortensis Thomas Hogg, a very free-flowering and welcome form; H. hortensis Mariesi, with large, soft-blue flowers tinged with pink, and often 3 inches across; H. hortensis mandschurica, and H. hortensis stellata flore-pleno, with partially double flowers, are worthy of attention.

H. PANICULATA.—Japan, 1874. This is one of the most distinct species, in which the flower-heads are elongated, not flat, as in most other species, and from which the finest form in cultivation has been obtained. This is H. paniculata grandiflora, in which the flowers are sterile and pure white, forming large panicles often a foot in length. It is a magnificent variety, and, being perfectly hardy, should be extensively planted for ornament. The flowers are produced in late summer, but remain in good form for fully two months, dying off a rich reddish hue.

H. QUERCIFOLIA. — Oak-leaved Hydrangea. Florida, 1803. This species has neatly-lobed leaves, and terminal panicles of pinky-white, but partially barren, flowers.

H. SCANDENS.—Climbing Hydrangea. Japan, 1879. This is not very hardy, but with the protection of a sunny wall it grows freely. The flowers are white.

The Hydrangeas require a rich, loamy soil, and, unless in maritime districts, a warm and sheltered situation. They are readily propagated by means of cuttings.

Hymenanthera (Violarieæ).

HYMENANTHERA CRASSIFOLIA.—A curious New Zealand (1875) shrub with rigid ashy-coloured branches, and small leathery entire leaves. The flowers are violet-like in colour, but by no means conspicuous. The small white berries which succeed the flowers are, in autumn, particularly attractive, and very ornamental. It is perfectly hardy, and of free growth in light peaty earth.

Hypericum (Hypericineæ).

HYPERICUM ANDROSÆMUM.—Tutsan, or Sweet Amber. Europe (Britain). A pretty native species, growing about 2 feet high, with ovate leaves having glandular dots and terminal clustered cymes of yellow flowers.

H. AUREUM.—South Carolina and Georgia, 1882. This soon forms a neat and handsome plant. The flowers are unusually large, and remarkable for the tufts of golden-yellow stamens with which they are furnished.

H. CALYCINUM.—Aaron's Beard, or Rose of Sharon. South-East Europe. This is a well-known species of shrubby growth, bearing large yellow flowers from 3 inches to 4 inches in diameter. It is a prostrate plant, with coriaceous glossy leaves with small pellucid dots, and of great value for planting in the shade, or on banks, where it spreads rapidly.

H. ELATUM is a spreading species from North America (1762), growing to fully 4 feet in height, and bearing terminal corymbs of large bright-yellow flowers in July and August. Leaves rather large, oblong-ovate, and revolute. On account of its spreading rapidly from the root, this species requires to be planted where it will have plenty of room.

H. HIRCINUM.—Goat-scented St. John's Wort. Mediterranean region, 1640. A small-growing and slender species, with oblong-lanceolate leaves 2 inches long, and producing yellow flowers in terminal heads. There is a smaller growing form known as H. hircinum minus. The plant emits a peculiar goat-like odour.

H. Moserianum is a beautiful hybrid form between H. calycinum and H. patulum, with large deep-yellow flowers and conspicuous red anthers.

H. oblongifolium (*syns H. Hookerianum* and *H. nepalensis*).—Nepaul, 1823. An evergreen species, about 4 feet high, with oblong, pellucid, dotted leaves, and deep golden, somewhat waxy flowers at the end of summer.

H. prolificum.—North America, 1758. This is a much branched twiggy shrub, about 4 feet high, with small, linear-lanceolate leaves, thickly studded with pellucid dots. Flowers not very large, five-petalled, and of a pleasing bright-yellow colour. The allied, if not identical, H. Kalmiana, North America, 1759, is worthy of being included in a selection of these plants.

H. uralum.—Nepaul, 1823. A neat but fragile species that attains to about a yard in height. Leaves rather small, elliptic, almost stalkless, and perforated with transparent dots. Flowers small and of a bright golden-yellow.

H. fasciculatum, H. pyramidatum, and H. patulum are all worthy of attention where a good representative collection is of importance. The Hypericums succeed best when planted in a rather sandy and not too dry loam, and they are readily increased either from divisions or by means of cuttings.

Idesia (Bixineæ).

Idesia polycarpa (*syns Flacourtica japonica* and *Polycarpa Maximowiczii*).—A Japanese tree of small growth, and only introduced to this country in 1866. It is a handsome, hardy species, bearing large bright-green leaves with conspicuous crimson footstalks, often 4 inches across, and of a glaucous tint on the undersides. The deliciously fragrant flowers are greenish-white or yellowish-green, and produced in graceful drooping racemes. In Southern England it does well, and, being a tree of unusual beauty of both leaves and flowers, is well worthy of attention. Rich loam, not too stiff, will grow the Idesia well.

I. POLYCARPA CRISPA is a distinct form in which the leaves are curiously crisped and cut.

Ilex (Ilicineæ).

ILEX AQUIFOLIUM.—Common Holly. Europe (Britain) and West Asia. Though the Hollies are not usually reckoned ornamental for the sake of their flowers, their berries are highly so. Some of them are nevertheless deliciously fragrant when in bloom. The leaves of this, our native species, in their typical form are oblong-ovate, wavy, and deeply spiny-toothed. The tree flowers in May and June, while the clusters of bright-red berries ripen in autumn, and persist all the winter, sometimes even hanging on the tree till a second crop is matured, provided they are not devoured by birds during severe weather. The varieties are very numerous, and differ chiefly in the form and toothing of the leaves, which are variegated in many cases, their size and form, and in the colour of the berries in a few instances.

I. Aquifolium albo-marginata has ovate, nearly flat, spiny-serrate leaves, with a narrow silvery margin, and fruits freely. I. Aquifolium fructu albo has white berries; in I. Aquifolium fructu luteo they are yellow and very abundantly produced; and in I. Aquifolium fructu nigro they are black. I. Aquifolium handsworthensis has elliptic-oblong spiny leaves, with a creamy-white margin and marbled with grey. Grafted trees bear berries in great profusion from the time they are only a foot high, and are highly ornamental. I. Aquifolium Hodginsii has large, broadly oblong-ovate, slightly spiny leaves, and large crimson-red berries that ripen late in autumn. I. Aquifolium Hodginsii aurea is a sub-variety with a broad golden margin to the leaves, and the disc splashed with grey. Beautiful and distinct is I. Aquifolium Lawsoniana, with ovate, flat, almost spineless leaves, heavily and irregularly blotched with yellow in the centre. The berries are of a brilliant red. The variety differs from Milkmaid in having flat, nearly entire leaves. I. Aquifolium pendula has a wide, rounded, drooping head, but otherwise does not differ from the type. Many others bear berries, but the above are all very distinct forms.

I. OPACA.—American Holly. United States, 1744. The leaves of this species are oblong or oval, small, spiny-serrate, and of a dark opaque green. The berries, which ripen in autumn, are small, bright red, and very liable to be eaten by birds. In America this Holly is put to precisely the same purposes as the common Holly is in Europe. It is perfectly hardy here.

Illicium (Magnoliaceæ).

ILLICIUM FLORIDANUM, from Florida (1771), is a beautiful but uncommon shrub, probably on account of its being tender and susceptible to injury by frost, unless in the warmer and more favoured parts of the country. The fragrant flowers are of a purplish-rose or deep red, while the foliage is neat and of a pleasing green.

I. ANISATUM (*syn I. religiosum*), from China and Japan (1842), with yellowish-white flowers and smooth, entire leaves, is too tender for outdoor culture in this country.

Indigofera (Leguminosæ).

INDIGOFERA GERARDIANA (*syn I. floribunda* and *I. Dosua*). —India, 1842. This forms a compact dwarf bush in the open, but is still better suited for covering a wall, the growth and floriferousness being then much increased. The foliage is neat and pea-green, while the bright-pink flowers are produced in long racemes. It is a pretty bush, and grows freely enough in any good garden soil, but very fine flowering specimens may be seen in light, sandy soil of a peaty nature. There is a white-flowered variety named I. Gerardiana alba. I. atropurpurea (Nepaul, 1816), with dark-purple and crimson flowers, is only half-hardy.

Itea (Saxifrageæ).

ITEA VIRGINICA.—North America, 1744. This is a neat, deciduous shrub of 6 feet or 8 feet in height. The ovate-lanceolate leaves are of a light greyish-green, turning deep red in autumn, and 3 inches to 5 inches long, and the small white flowers are produced in dense racemes in June. Planted in a somewhat shady place, and in rather cool, damp soil, this little shrub does well and flowers profusely.

Jamesia (Saxifrageæ).

JAMESIA AMERICANA.—Rocky Mountains and Colorado, 1865. Amongst early spring-flowering shrubs this pretty but neglected plant is one of the best, of perfect hardihood, for it stands the vigour of our winters with impunity, and of dense thick growth; it is suitable for using in a variety of ways, as well as for purely ornamental purposes. The leaves are oval and neatly dentated, and the flowers individually of large size, pure white, and produced in terminal bunches in June. Cool soil and a shady situation would seem to suit this shrub admirably, but for screen purposes in the rock garden or border it is invaluable on account of the strong and dense twigs.

Jasminum (Oleaceæ).

JASMINUM FRUTICANS.—South Europe, 1570. An evergreen species, well adapted, from its rather stiff and upright growth, for planting alone. It has angular branches, trifoliate leaves, and showy yellow flowers.

J. HUMILE.—India, 1656. A hardy species of dwarf growth, with angular branches, and bearing beautiful golden flowers in summer.

J. NUDIFLORUM.—Naked Jasmine. China, 1844. A showy and well-known species, from China, with numerous, usually solitary yellow flowers, ternate leaves, and flexible branches. The variety J. nudiflorum aureo-variegatum has golden-variegated leaves.

J. OFFICINALE.—Northern India to Persia, 1548. The white-flowered Jasmine of our gardens is a very beautiful and desirable clambering shrub, either for wall covering, for planting by tree stumps, rooteries, or rockeries, or for screening and draping the pergola or garden lattice-work. From its great hardihood, vigour of growth, and beauty of flowers, it is certainly one of the most deservedly popular of wall shrubs. The branches are deep green, angular, and flexible, the leaves pinnate, and the flowers pure white and sweetly scented. The variety J. officinale affine has flowers that are individually larger than those of the species; J. officinale aurea has badly-variegated leaves; J. officinale grandiflorum and J. officinale grandiflorum majus are also desirable kinds.

J. PUBIGERUM GLABRUM (*syn J. Wallichianum*), from North-West India, is not well known, being tender in most parts of the country.

J. REVOLUTUM.—India, 1812. This has persistent, dark glossy-green leaves, and fragrant, bright-yellow flowers, produced in large terminal clusters. From India, but perfectly hardy as a wall plant, for which purpose, with its bright evergreen leaves, it is well suited.

As regards soil, the Jasmines are very accommodating, and are propagated by layers or cuttings.

Kadsura (Magnoliaceæ).

KADSURA JAPONICA.—Japan, 1846. This is a small-growing shrub, with lanceolate and pointed leaves that are remotely dentated. The flowers are not very showy, being of a yellowish-white colour about an inch across, and produced from June to September. They are borne both terminal and axillary, and in fair abundance. The scarlet fruits are arranged in clusters, and when fully ripe are both showy and interesting. Generally speaking this shrub suffers from severe frost, but as only the branch tips are injured, it shoots freely from the stock. There is a variety with variegated leaves, both succeeding in light, loamy soil.

Kalmia (Ericaceæ).

KALMIA ANGUSTIFOLIA.—Sheep Laurel. Canada, 1736. This is at once distinguished from K. latifolia by its much smaller and narrower leaves and smaller crimson or purple flowers, these also being of brighter tint and more plentifully produced. It rarely exceeds 2 feet in height. Of this there are two very distinct forms, that named K. angustifolia pumila, of neat and dense growth; and K. angustifolia rubra, in which the flowers are of an unusually deep-red colour.

K. CUNEATA.—North Carolina, 1820. (Reintroduced about 1896.) This is of low growth, about 2 feet, with oblong, wedge-shaped leaves and corymbs of white flowers with a red band at the base of the limb, and produced in May.

K. GLAUCA.—Canada and Sitcha, 1767. This, which has lilac-purple flowers fully half an inch in diameter, produced in early spring, is not a very desirable species, being of rather straggling growth and with few flowers.

K. HIRSUTA.—Hairy-leaved Kalmia. South-East Virginia to Florida, 1786. This is at once distinguished by the rather rough and hairy foliage and few rosy-tinted flowers. It is of dwarf, neat growth.

K. LATIFOLIA.—Calico Bush, or Mountain Laurel. Alleghanies, Canada, and Western Florida, 1734. A favourite shrub in every garden where the conditions of soil will allow of its being successfully cultivated. In peaty soil, or light, friable loam and leaf soil, it forms a dense, round-headed bush, often 8 feet in height, and nearly as much through, with pleasing green leaves and dense clusters of beautiful pink, wax-like flowers. The flowering period commences in May, and usually extends to the end of July. This is a choice shrub of great hardihood, and one of the handsomest flowering in cultivation. There is a still more beautiful form named K. latifolia major splendens, and one with small Myrtle-like foliage named K. latifolia myrtifolia; while K. latifolia Pavarti (1888) has very bright-coloured flowers, and is a desirable variety.

The members of this handsome family are, as a rule, partial to cool, damp soil, peat of a light, sandy nature being preferred. They thrive well where Azaleas and Rhododendrons will succeed. In bold masses they have a fine effect, but a well-developed standard specimen of the commonly cultivated species is highly ornamental.

Kerria (Rosaceæ).

KERRIA JAPONICA (*syn Corchorus japonicus*).—Japan, 1700. A Japanese shrub, the double-flowered variety of which, K. japonica flore-pleno, is one of our commonest wall plants. The orange-yellow flowers, produced in great rosettes, are highly ornamental, and have earned for the shrub a well-known name. It succeeds well almost anywhere, and, though usually seen as a wall plant, is perfectly hardy, and forms a neat shrub for the open border. There is a form in which the leaves are variegated, and known under the name of K. japonica variegata.

Kœlreuteria (Sapindaceæ).

KŒLREUTERIA PANICULATA. — Northern China, 1763. Whether for its foliage or flowers, this small-growing tree is worthy of a place. Though of rather irregular growth, the beautiful foliage and large panicles of yellowish flowers, which stand well above the leaves, make the shrub (for it does not in this country attain to tree height) one of particular interest, and a valuable aid in ornamental planting. In a sheltered corner, and planted in rich soil, it grows and flowers freely.

Laburnum (Leguminosæ).

LABURNUM ADAMI (*syn Cytisus Adami*).—A graft hybrid form between the common Laburnum and Cytisus purpureus, the result being flowers of the Laburnum, the true Cytisus purpureus, and the graft hybrid between the two. It was raised by Jean Louis Adam in 1825. It is a curious and distinct tree, worthy of culture if only for the production of three distinct kinds of flowers on the same plant.

L. ALPINUM (*syn Cytisus alpinus*).—Scotch Laburnum. Europe, 1596. This very closely resembles the common Laburnum, but it is of larger growth, and flowers later in the season. The flowers, too, though in longer racemes, are usually less plentifully produced and with a shorter fruit pod. It grows 30 feet high. There is a weeping form, L. alpinum pendulum, and another with fragrant flowers, named L. alpinum fragrans, as also a third, with very long racemes of flowers, named L. alpinum Alschingeri.

L. CARAMANICUM.—Asia Minor, 1879. A bushy shrub of vigorous habit, with trifoliate and petiolate leaves of a pale-green colour, thick and tough, and brightly polished on the upper surface. Flowers bright yellow, the calyx being helmet-shaped and rusty-red. It is a beautiful but uncommon shrub, and succeeds very well in chalky or calcareous soil. Flowers in July.

L. VULGARE (*syn Cytisus Laburnum*).—Common Laburnum. Southern France to Hungary, 1596. This is one of our commonest garden and park trees, and at the same time one of the most beautiful and floriferous. The large, pendulous racemes of bright-yellow flowers are, when at their best in May, surpassed neither in quantity nor beauty by those of any other hardy tree. There are several varieties of this Laburnum—a few good, but many worthless, at least from a garden point of view. L. vulgare Parkesii is a seedling form, raised in 1840, bearing large racemes of deep-coloured flowers, often 14 inches long; L. vulgare Watereri was raised in the Knap Hill Nursery, Surrey, and is one of the most distinct and beautiful of the many forms into which the Laburnum has been subdivided. The flower racemes are very long and richly coloured. L. vulgare quercifolium and L. vulgare sessilifolium are fairly well described by their names; L. vulgare fragrans differs only in having sweetly-scented flowers; L. vulgare involutum has curiously-curled leaves; while L. vulgare aureum, where it does well, is a beautiful and distinct form, with golden-yellow leaves.

Lapageria (Liliaceæ).

LAPAGERIA ROSEA.—Chili, 1847. This is, unfortunately, not hardy, unless in favoured maritime districts, but in such situations it has stood unharmed for many years, and attained to goodly proportions. It is a beautiful climber, with deep-green lanceolate-ovate leaves, and large, fleshy, campanulate flowers of a deep rose colour. There is a white-flowered form called L. alba, introduced from Chili in 1854, and a beautiful crimson-flowered variety named superba. Planted on an east aspect wall, and in roughly broken up peat and gritty sand, it succeeds well.

Lardizabala (Berberideæ).

LARDIZABALA BITERNATA.—Chili, 1848. Requires wall protection, there being few situations in which it will succeed when planted in the open. It is a tall, climbing shrub, with dark-green persistent leaves, and bearing purplish flowers in drooping racemes in mid-winter. Planted in rather dry soil, at the base of a sunny wall, this shrub forms a by no means unattractive covering, the twice ternate, glossy leaves being fresh and beautiful the winter through.

Lavandula (Labiatæ).

LAVANDULA VERA (*syn L. Spica*).—Common Lavender. South Europe, 1568. A well-known and useful plant, but of no particular value for ornamental purposes. It is of shrubby growth, with narrow-lanceolate, hoary leaves, and terminal spikes of blue flowers. Good loam suits it well.

Lavatera (Malvaceæ).

LAVATERA ARBOREA.—Tree Mallow. Coasts of Europe (Britain). A stout-growing shrub reaching in favourable situations a height of fully 6 feet, with broadly orbicular leaves placed on long stalks. The flowers are plentiful and showy, of a pale purplish-red colour, and collected into clusters. It is a seaside shrub, succeeding best in sheltered maritime recesses, and when in full flower is one of the most ornamental of our native plants. There is also a beautiful variegated garden form, L. a. variegata.

Ledum (Ericaceæ).

LEDUM LATIFOLIUM (*syn L. grœnlandicum*).—Wild Rosemary, or Labrador Tea. United States, 1763. This is a small shrub, reaching to about 3 feet in height, indigenous to swampy ground in Canada, Greenland, and over a large area of the colder parts of America. Leaves oval or oblong, and plentifully produced all over the plant. Flowers pure white, or slightly tinted with pink, produced in terminal corymbs, and usually at their best in April. A perfectly hardy, neat-growing, and abundantly-flowered shrub, but one that, somehow, has gone greatly out of favour in this country. This plant has been sub-divided into several varieties, that are, perhaps, distinct enough to render them worthy of attention. They are L. latifolium globosum, with white flowers, borne in globose heads, on the short, twiggy, and dark-foliaged branches. L. latifolium angustifolia has narrower leaves than those of the species, while L. latifolium intermedium is of neat growth and bears pretty, showy flowers.

L. PALUSTRE.—Marsh Ledum (1762). This is a common European species, growing from 2 feet to 3 feet high, with much smaller leaves than the former, and small pinky-white flowers produced in summer. It is an interesting and pretty plant. The Ledums succeed best in cool, damp, peaty soil.

Leiophyllum (Ericaceæ).

LEIOPHYLLUM BUXIFOLIUM (*syns L. thymifolia, Ammyrsine buxifolia* and *Ledum buxifolium*).—Sand Myrtle. New Jersey and Virginia, 1736. This is a dwarf, compact shrub, with box-like leaves, and bunches of small white flowers with pinky tips in early summer. For using as a rock plant, and in sandy peat, it is an excellent subject, and should find a place in every collection.

Lespedeza (Leguminosæ).

LESPEDEZA BICOLOR (*syn Desmodium penduliflorum*).—North China and Japan. A little-known but beautiful small-growing shrub of slender, elegant growth, and reaching, under favourable culture, a height of about 6 feet. The leaves are trifoliate, small, and neat, and the abundant racemes of individually small, pea-shaped flowers are of the richest and showiest reddish- or rosy-purple. Being only semi-hardy will probably account for the scarcity of this beautiful Japanese shrub. It has, however, stood uninjured in all but the coldest parts of these islands, which should induce lovers of flowering shrubs to give it a fair trial. L. bicolor flore alba (1893) is a white-flowered variety.

Leucothoë (Ericaceæ).

LEUCOTHOE AXILLARIS (*syn Andromeda axillaris*).—North America, 1765. This is of small growth, from 2 feet to 3 feet high, with oval-pointed leaves and white flowers in short racemes produced in May and June. It is not a very satisfactory species for cultivation in this country.

L. CATESBÆI (*syn Andromeda Catesbœi* and *A. axillaris*).—North America. This has white flowers with an unpleasant odour like that of Chestnut blossoms, but is worthy of cultivation, and succeeds best in cool sandy peat or friable yellow loam.

L. DAVISIÆ, from California (1853), is a very handsome evergreen shrub, of small, neat growth, and will be found an acquisition where compact growing specimens are in demand. The leaves are small, of a deep-green colour, and remain throughout the year. Flowers produced in great abundance at the branch tips, usually in dense clusters, and individually small and pure white.

L. RECURVA (*syn Andromeda recurva*).—North America. A very distinct plant on account of the branch tips being almost of a scarlet tint, and thus affording a striking contrast to the greyish-green of the older bark. The flowers are pinky-white and produced in curving racemes abundantly over the shrub. Like other members of the family it delights to grow in cool sandy peat. L. acuminata (North America, 1765) has white flowers in great profusion, and L. racemosa bears spikes of white flowers, mostly solitary.

Leycesteria (Caprifoliaceæ).

LEYCESTERIA FORMOSA, from Nepaul (1824), is an erect-growing, deciduous shrub, with green, hollow stems, and large ovate, pointed leaves of a very deep-green colour. The flowers are small, white or purplish, and produced in long, pendulous, bracteate racemes from the axils of the upper leaves. It is one of the most distinct and interesting of hardy shrubs, the deep olive-green of both stem and leaves, and abundantly-produced and curiously-shaped racemes, rendering it a conspicuous object wherever planted. Perfectly hardy, and of free, almost rampant growth in any but the stiffest soils. Cuttings root freely and grow rapidly. There is a variegated variety named L. formosa variegata.

Ligustrina. See Syringa.

Ligustrum (Oleaceæ).

LIGUSTRUM IBOTA (*syn L. amurense*).—Japan, 1861. A compact growing species, about 3 feet in height, with small spikes of pure-white salver-shaped flowers produced freely during the summer months.

L. JAPONICUM (*syns L. glabrum, L. Kellermanni, L. Sieboldii* and *L. syringæflorum*).—Japan Privet. 1845. This is a dwarf-growing species rarely exceeding 4 feet in height, with broad, smooth, glossy-green leaves,.and large compound racemes of white, slightly fragrant flowers. There are several varieties, including L. japonicum microphyllum, with smaller leaves than the parent; and one with tri-coloured foliage named L. japonicum variegatum.

L. LUCIDUM (*syns L. magnoliæfolium* and *L. strictum*).—Shining-leaved Privet, or Woa Tree. China, 1794. A pretty evergreen species, with oval leaves, and terminal, thyrsoid panicles of white or yellowish-white flowers. It is an old inhabitant of our gardens, and forms a somewhat erect, twiggy bush, of fully 10 feet in height. Of this there are two varieties, one with larger bunches of flowers, named L. lucidum floribundum, and another with variegated leaves, L. lucidum variegatum. L. lucidum coriaceum (Leathery-leaved Privet) is a distinct variety, with thick, leathery-green leaves, and dense habit of growth.

L. MEDIUM.—Japan, 1891. This has broadly lanceolate acute leaves and small white flowers.

L. OVALIFOLIUM (*syn L. californicum*).—Oval-leaved Privet. Japan, 1877. This is a commonly cultivated species, with semi-evergreen leaves, and spikes of yellowish-white flowers. It is a good hedge plant, and succeeds well as a town shrub. There are several variegated forms, of which L. ovalifolium variegatum (Japan, 1865) and L. ovalifolium aureum are the best.

L. QUIHOI.—China, 1868. This is a much valued species, as it does not flower until many of its relations have finished. Most of the Privets flower at mid-summer, but this species is often only at its best by the last week of October and beginning of November. It forms a straggling, freely-branched shrub, of fully 6 feet in height and nearly as much through, with dark shining-green oblong leaves, and loose terminal panicles of pure-white, powerfully-scented flowers. It flourishes, like most of the Privets, on poor soil, and is a little-known species that note should be made of during the planting season.

L. SINENSE (*syns L. villosum* and *L. Ibota villosum*).—Chinese Privet. China, 1874. This is a tall deciduous shrub, with oblong and tomentose leaves, and small white flowers in loose, terminal panicles produced freely in August. L. sinense nanum is one of the prettiest forms in cultivation. It is almost evergreen, with a horizontal mode of growth, and dense spikes of creamy-white flowers, so thickly produced as almost to hide the foliage from view. It is a most distinct and desirable variety.

L. VULGARE.—Common Privet. Europe, North Africa: Although one of our commonest shrubs, this Privet can hardly be passed unnoticed, for the spikes of creamy-white flowers, that are deliciously scented, are both handsome and effective. Of the common Privet there are several distinct and highly ornamental forms, such as L. vulgare variegatum, L. vulgare pendulum, having curiously-creeping branches, and the better-known and valuable L. vulgare sempervirens (*syn L. italicum*), the Italian Privet.

Linnæa (Caprifoliaceæ).

LINNÆA BOREALIS.—Twin Flower. A small and elegant, much-creeping evergreen shrub, with ovate crenate leaves, and pairs of very fragrant pink flowers in May and June. Two conditions are necessary for its cultivation—a half-shaded aspect where bottom moisture is always present, and a deep, rich, friable loam. A native of Scotland and England

Linum (Lineæ).

Linum arboreum.—Greece, 1788. A neat-habited, small-growing shrub which produces plentifully in early summer its golden flowers. Being an evergreen, and rarely exceeding 18 inches in height, it is well suited for pot culture, and succeeds in any free, light soil.

Lippia (Verbenaceæ).

Lippia citriodora (*syns Aloysia citriodora* and *Verbena triphylla*).—Lemon-scented Verbena. Chili, 1794. With its slender branches and pale-green, pleasantly-scented, linear leaves, this little plant is a general favourite that needs no description. The flowers are not very ornamental, being white or lilac, and produced in small, terminal panicles. A native of Chili, it is not very hardy, but grown against a sunny wall, and afforded the protection of a mat in winter, with a couple of shovelfuls of cinders heaped around the stem, it passes through the most severe weather with little or no injury, save, in some instances, the branch tips being killed back. As a pot or tub shrub it does well. Propagated readily from cuttings placed in a cool frame or under a hand-light.

Liriodendron (Magnoliaceæ).

Liriodendron tulipifera.—Tulip Tree. North America, 1688. One of the noblest hardy exotic trees in cultivation. The large, four-lobed, truncate leaves, of a soft and pleasing green, are highly ornamental, and are alone sufficient to establish the identity of the tree. Flowers large, yellow, variegated with green and orange, and sweet-scented, and usually freely produced when the tree has attained to a height of between 20 feet and 30 feet. When we consider the undoubted hardihood of the tree and indifference to soil, its noble aspect, handsome foliage that is so distinct from that of any other tree, and showy flowers, we feel justified in placing it in the very first rank of ornamental trees. L. tulipifera integrifolia has entire leaves, which render it distinct from the type; L. tulipifera fastigiata, or pyramidalis, is of erect growth; L. tulipifera aurea, with golden foliage; and L. tulipifera crispa, with the leaves curiously undulated—a peculiarity which seems constant, but is more curious than beautiful. Few soils come amiss to the Tulip Tree, it thriving well in that of very opposite descriptions—loam, almost pure gravel, and alluvial deposit.

Loiseleurea. See Rhododendron.

Lomatia (Proteaceæ).

LOMATIA FERRUGINEA.—Chili, 1851. A well-rounded, highly-ornamental shrub with pinnate foliage and an abundance of brownish-red flowers. Heretofore it has been considered as only half-hardy, but having stood unharmed in Ireland for about twenty years, its adaptability to the warmer parts of Britain is insured. Rich soil composed of fibrous peat and loam will suit it well.

Lonicera (Caprifoliaceæ).

LONICERA CAPRIFOLIUM.—Europe. This species resembles L. Periclymenum, but is readily distinguished by the sessile flower-heads and fawny-orange flowers.

L. FLEXUOSA (*syn L. brachypoda*).—Japan, 1806. This is a pretty species, and one of the most useful of the climbing section. By its slender, twining, purplish stems, it may at once be distinguished, as also by the deep-green, purplish-tinted leaves and sweetly-scented flowers of various shades of yellow and purple. A native of China and Japan, and perfectly hardy as a wall or pillar plant. L. flexuosa aureo-reticulata is a worthy variety, in which the leaves are beautifully netted or variegated with yellow.

L. FRAGRANTISSIMA.—China, 1845. This species is often confounded with L. Standishii, but differs in at least one respect, that the former is strictly a climber, while the latter is of bushy growth. The leaves, too, of L. Standishii are hairy, which is not the case with the other species. It is a very desirable shrub, with white fragrant flowers, produced during the winter season.

L. HISPIDA (Siberia, 1883) has greenish-white pendulous flowers, ovate-elliptical leaves, and erect stems growing to about a yard in height.

L. PERICLYMENUM.—Honeysuckle, or Woodbine. An indigenous climbing shrub, with long, lithe, and twisted cable-like branches, and bearing heads of sweetly-scented reddish-yellow flowers. This is a favourite wild plant, and in the profusion and fragrance of its flowers it is surpassed by none of the exotic species. There are several distinct nursery forms of this plant, including those known as L. Periclymenum Late Dutch, L. Periclymenum Early Cream, and L. Periclymenum odoratissimum; as also one with variegated foliage.

L. SEMPERVIRENS.—Scarlet Trumpet Honeysuckle. A North American evergreen species (1656), with scarlet, almost inodorous flowers, produced freely during the summer. For wall covering it is one of the most useful of the family. The variety L. sempervirens minor is worthy of attention.

L. STANDISHII, a Chinese species (1860), has deliciously-fragrant white flowers, with a slight purplish tint, and is well worthy of attention, it soon forming a wall covering of great beauty.

L. TATARICA.—Tartarian Honeysuckle. Tartary, 1752.

This is a very variable species, in so far at least as the colour of flowers is concerned, and has given rise to several handsome varieties. The typical plant has rosy flowers, but the variety L. tatarica albiflora has pure-white flowers; and another, L. tatarica rubiflora has freely-produced purplish-red flowers.

L. TRAGOPHYLLA (China) is a rare species in cultivation, but one of the most ornamental of the genus. It has large entire leaves, fully 3 inches long, with golden-yellow flowers, which turn reddish with advance of age. So far it has proved hardy.

L. XYLOSTEUM (*syn Xylosteum dumetorum*).—Fly Honeysuckle. Europe (England) to the Caucasus. The small, creamy-white flowers of this plant are not particularly showy, but the scarlet berries are more conspicuous in September and October. The grey bark of the branches has also a distinct effect in winter when grown in contrast to the red-barked species of Cornus, Viburnum, and yellow-barked Osier. It is one of the oldest occupants of British shrubberies. L. Xylosteum leucocarpum has white berries; those of L. Xylosteum melanocarpum are black; and in L. Xylosteum xanthocarpum they are yellow.

The Honeysuckles are all of the readiest culture, and succeed well in very poor soils, and in that of opposite qualities. Propagated from cuttings or by layering.

Loropetalum (Hamamelideæ).

LOROPETALUM CHINENSE.—Khasia Mountains and China, 1880. This is a pretty and interesting shrub belonging to the more familiar Witch Hazel family. Flowers clustered in small heads, the calyx pale green, and the long linear petals almost pure white. Being quite hardy and interesting as well as ornamental, should insure this Chinese shrub a place in every good collection.

Lycium (Solanaceæ).

Lycium barbarum.—Box Thorn, or Tea Tree. North Asia, 1696. A pretty lax, trailing shrub, with long, slender, flexible twigs, small linear-lanceolate leaves, and rather sparsely-produced lilac or violet flowers. Planted against a wall, or beside a stout-growing, open-habited shrub, where the peculiarly lithe branches can find support, this plant does best. Probably nowhere is the Box Thorn so much at home as in seaside places, it then attaining to sometimes 12 feet in height, and bearing freely its showy flowers during summer, and the bright scarlet or orange berries in winter.

L. europæum.—European Box Thorn. South Europe, 1730. This is a spiny, rambling shrub, that may often be seen clambering over some cottage porch, or used as a fence or wall plant in many parts of England. It often grows nearly 20 feet long, and is then a plant of great beauty, with linear-spathulate leaves of the freshest green, and pretty little pink or reddish flowers. For quickly covering steep, dry banks and mounds where few other plants could exist, this European Box Thorn is invaluable. Either species will grow in very poor, dry soil, and is readily propagated by means of cuttings.

L. pallidum (Arizona, 1888) has green or purple-tinged flowers and showy bright red fruit.

Lyonia (Eriçaceæ).

Lyonia paniculata (*syns L. ligustrina, Andromeda globulifera, A. pilifera,* and *Menziesia globularis*).—North America, 1806. This species grows about a yard high, with clustered ovate leaves, and pretty, pinky-white, drooping flowers. Sandy peat will suit it.

Maclura (Urticaceæ).

MACLURA AURANTIACA.—Osage Orange, or Bow-wood. North America, 1818. This is a wide-spreading tree with deciduous foliage, and armed with spines along the branches. The leaves are 3 inches long, ovate and pointed, and of a bright shining green. Flowers rather inconspicuous, being green with a light tinge of yellow, and succeeded by fruit bearing a resemblance when ripe to the Seville orange. It is hardy, and grows freely in rather sandy or gravelly soil.

Magnolia (Magnoliaceæ).

MAGNOLIA ACUMINATA.—Cucumber Tree. North America, 1736. This is a large and handsome species, of often as much as 50 feet in height, and with a head that is bushy in proportion. The leaves are 6 inches long, ovate and pointed, and of a refreshing shade of green. Flowers greenish-yellow, sweetly scented, and produced abundantly all over the tree from May to July. They are succeeded by small, roughish fruit, resembling an infant cucumber, but they usually fall off before becoming ripe.

M. CAMPBELLII.—Sikkim, 1868. This is a magnificent Indian species, but, unfortunately, it is not hardy except in the favoured English and Irish localities. The leaves are large, and silky on the undersides, while the flowers are crimson and white, and equally as large as those of the better-known M. grandiflora.

M. CONSPICUA (*syn M. Yulan*).—Yulan. China, 1789. A large-growing shrub, with pea-green deciduous foliage, and large, pure-white fragrant flowers that oft get damaged by the spring frosts. M. conspicua Soulangeana is a supposed hybrid between M. conspicua and M. obovata. Whatever may be the origin of this Magnolia, it is certainly a handsome and showy plant of very vigorous growth, producing freely its white, purple-tinted flowers, which last for a long time in perfection. There are several other varieties, including M. conspicua Soulangeana nigra, with dark purplish flowers ; M. conspicua Alexandrina, M. conspicua Soulangeana speciosa, and M. conspicua Norbertii.

M. CORDATA, a native of the Southern Alleghanies (1801), is still rare in collections. It is a small-growing, deciduous species, with heart-shaped leaves and yellow flowers, that are neither scented nor showy.

M. FRASERI (*syn M. auriculata*).—Long-leaved Cucumber Tree. North America, 1786. This species has distinctly auriculated leaves, that are often a foot long, and large, yellowish-white, fragrant flowers.

M. GLAUCA.—Laurel Magnolia. North America, 1688. This is one of the commonest species in our gardens, and at the same time one of the hardiest. It is of shrub size, with Laurel-like leaves, and sweetly-scented, small, pure-white flowers produced about the end of June. M. glauca major has flowers and leaves nearly three times larger than those of the species. It is synonymous with M. Thompsoniana.

M. GRANDIFLORA.—North America, 1737. One of the handsomest species, with very large, glossy, evergreen leaves, and deliciously oduriferous, creamy-white flowers that are often fully 6 inches across. It is usually seen as a wall plant, and the slight protection thus afforded is almost a necessity in so far as the development of the foliage and flowers is concerned. M. grandiflora exoniensis (Exmouth Magnolia) is a very handsome form.

M. HYPOLEUCA.—Japan, 1893. This has large leaves, about 15 inches long and 8 inches wide, and creamy-white flowers with purple anthers, which measure 7 inches across. It is a noble-growing species that succeeds well in strong loam by the side of a stream or pond.

M. KOBUS (Japan) is another new and desirable species with creamy-white, six-petalled flowers and a neat habit of growth. The leaves often measure 7 inches long by 3 inches broad.

M. Lenné.—This is a garden hybrid between M. conspicua and M. obovata discolor, and has flowers as large as a goose's egg, of a rosy-purple colour, and produced profusely.

M. macrophylla.—North America, 1800. This species has very large leaves; and flowers larger, perhaps, than those of any other Magnolia, being from 8 inches to 10 inches in diameter. They are very showy, and white with a purple centre. It attains a height of 30 feet.

M. obovata discolor (*syn M. purpurea*).—Japan, 1790. This is a small-growing, deciduous shrub, with large, dark-green leaves and tulip-shaped flowers that are purple on the outside and almost white within.

M. parviflora, from Japan, with creamy-white, fragrant flowers, that are globular in shape, is a very distinct and attractive species, but cannot generally be relied upon as hardy.

M. stellata (*syn M. Halleana*).—Japan, 1878. A neat, small-growing, Japanese species, of bushy habit, and quite hardy in this country. The small, white, fragrant flowers are produced abundantly, even on young plants, and as early as April. One of the most desirable and handsome of the small-growing species. M. stellata rosea (pink variety) received an Award of Merit at the meeting of the Royal Horticultural Society on March 28, 1893. This bids fair to be really a good thing, and may best be described as a pink-flowered form of the now well-known and popular species.

M. Umbrella (*syn M. tripetala*).—Umbrella Tree. North America, 1752. A noble species, with large, deep-green leaves that are often 16 inches long. It is quite hardy around London, and produces its large, white, fragrant flowers in succession during May and June. The fruit is large and showy, and of a deep purplish-red colour.

M. WIESNERI.—Japan, 1899. This is a dwarf bush, with long, thick leaves and sweetly-scented flowers.

Two recently introduced species from China and Japan are M. salicifolia, with willow-like leaves; and M. Watsoni, with fragrant flowers, which are cream-coloured with red stamens, and leaves often 6 inches in length, the flowers and leaves being produced at the same time.

The Magnolias thrive best in a warm, sheltered situation and in light, rich soil. They are impatient of root disturbance.

Mahonia. See Berberis.

Malachodendron. See Stuartia.

Medicago (Leguminosæ).

MEDICAGO ARBOREA.—South Europe, 1596. This species grows to the height of 6 feet or 8 feet, and produces its racemes of yellow pea-shaped flowers from June onwards. The leaves are broadly oval and serrated at the tips, but they vary in this respect. It is not hardy unless in warm, sheltered corners of Southern England and Ireland, although it stood unharmed for many years at Kew. It succeeds best, and is less apt to receive injury, when planted in rather dry and warm soil.

Menispermum (Menispermaceæ).

MENISPERMUM CANADENSE.—Moonseed. North America, 1691. This shrub is principally remarkable for the large, reniform, peltate leaves, which are of value for covering pergolas, bowers, and walls. The yellowish, paniculate flowers are of no great account, being rather inconspicuous. It is hardy in most places, and is worthy of culture for its graceful habit and handsome foliage.

Menziesia. See Daboëcia and Phyllodoce.

Mespilus. See Pyrus, Photinia, and Cratægus.

Microglossa (Compositæ).

MICROGLOSSA ALBESCENS (*syn Aster albescens* and *A. cabulicus*).—Himalayas, 1842. This member of the Compositæ family is a much-branched shrub, with greyish lanceolate foliage and clusters of flowers about 6 inches in diameter and of a bluish or mauve colour. It is a native of Nepaul, and, with the protection of a wall, perfectly hardy around London.

Mitchella (Rubiaceæ).

MITCHELLA REPENS.—Partridge Berry. North America, 1761. A low-growing, creeping plant, having oval, persistent leaves, whitish-purple flowers, and brilliant scarlet fruit. It is a neat little bog plant, resembling Fuchsia procumbens in habit, and with bunches of the brightest Cotoneaster-like fruit. For rock gardening, or planting on the margins of beds in light, peaty soil, this is one of the handsomest and most beautiful of hardy creeping shrubs.

Mitraria (Gesneraceæ).

MITRARIA COCCINEA.—Scarlet Mitre Pod. Chiloe, 1848. This is only hardy in the South of England and Ireland, and even there it requires wall protection. It is a pretty little shrub, with long, slender shoots, which, during the early part of the summer, are studded with the bright-red, drooping blossoms, which are urn-shaped, and often nearly 2 inches long. It delights in damp, lumpy peat and sand.

Myrica (Myricaceæ).

Myrica asplenifolia (*syn Comptonia asplenifolia*).—Sweet Fern. North America, 1714. This is a plant of somewhat straggling growth, growing to about 4 feet high, and with linear, pinnatified, sweet-smelling leaves. The flowers are of no decorative value, being small and inconspicuous, but for the fragrant leaves alone the shrub will always be prized. It grows well in peaty soil, is very hardy, and may be increased by means of offsets. This shrub is nearly allied to our native Myrica, or Sweet Gale.

M. californica.—Californian Wax Myrtle. California, 1848. In this we have a valuable evergreen shrub that is hardy beyond a doubt, and that will thrive in the very poorest classes of soils. In appearance it somewhat resembles our native plant, but is preferable to it on account of the deep-green, persistent leaves. The leaves are about 3 inches long, narrow, and produced in tufts along the branches, while the flowers are greenish-white. Unlike our native species, the Californian Wax Myrtle has no pleasant aroma to the leaves.

M. cerifera.—Common Candle-berry Myrtle. Canada, 1699. This is a neat little shrub, usually about 4 feet high, with oblong-lanceolate leaves, and inconspicuous reddish catkins.

M. Gale.—Sweet Gale or Bog Myrtle. This has inconspicuous brownish-green flowers, and is included here on account of the deliciously fragrant foliage, which makes it a favourite with cultivators generally. It is a native shrub, growing from 3 feet to 4 feet high, with deciduous, linear-lanceolate leaves, and clustered catkins appearing before the leaves. A moor or bog plant, and of great value for planting by the pond or lake side, or along with the so-called American plants, for the aroma given off by the foliage.

The Myricas are all worthy of cultivation, although the flowers are inconspicuous—their neat and, in most cases, fragrant foliage, and adaptability to poor, dampish soil, being extra recommendations.

Myricaria (Tamariscineæ).

Myricaria germanica.—Europe, Asia, 1582. A tall, somewhat straggling shrub, very similar to the Tamarisk, with terminal spikes of pink or rosy flowers, produced freely nearly all the summer. It succeeds well in this country in seaside situations, and is often described as a Tamarisk by gardeners. Any free soil will suit.

Myrtus (Myrtaceæ).

Myrtus communis.—Common Myrtle. South Europe, 1597. A well-known shrub, which, unless in very favoured spots and by the seaside, cannot survive our winters. Where it does well, and then only as a wall plant, this and its varieties are charming shrubs with neat foliage and an abundance of showy white flowers. The double-flowered varieties are very handsome, but they are more suitable for glass culture than planting in the open.

M. Luma (*syn Eugenia apiculata* and *E. Luma*).—Chili. Though sometimes seen growing out of doors, this is not to be recommended for general planting, it being best suited for greenhouse culture. The flowers are large and white.

M. Ugni (*syn Eugenia Ugni*).—Valdivia, 1845. A small-growing, Myrtle-like shrub, that is only hardy in favoured parts of the country. It is of branching habit, with small, wiry stems, oval, coriacious leaves, and pretty pinky-white flowers. The edible fruit is highly ornamental, being of a pleasing ruddy tinge tinted with white. This dwarf-growing shrub wants the protection of a wall, and when so situated in warm seaside parts of the country soon forms a bush of neat and pleasing appearance. They succeed best in sandy peat.

Nandina (Berberideæ).

NANDINA DOMESTICA.—China and Japan, 1804. Not generally hardy, but succeeding in several of the milder parts of England and Wales. It grows from 4 feet to 6 feet in height, with pinnate leaves, which in a young state are tinted with red, and trusses of individually small white flowers in summer. On gravelly subsoil and planted in light loam and a warm situation we have found it to do best.

Neillia (Rosaceæ).

NEILLIA AMURENSIS (*syn Spiræa amurensis*).—Amurland. This has roundish, lobed leaves with toothed margins and white flowers. It attains a height of about 6 feet, and succeeds well in light, warm loam, and in a position sheltered from cold winds.

N. OPULIFOLIA (*syn Spiræa opulifolia*).—Nine Bark. North America, 1690. A hardy shrub, nearly allied to Spiræa. It produces a profusion of umbel-like corymbs of pretty white flowers, that are succeeded by curious swollen membraneous purplish fruit. N. opulifolia aurea is worthy of culture, it being of free growth and distinct from the parent plant in the foliage being of a rich golden tint.

N. THYRSIFLORA (Nepaul, 1850) would seem to be quite as hardy as N. opulifolia, and is of more evergreen habit. The leaves are cordate-ovate, doubly serrated, and three lobed. Flowers white in spicate, thyrsoid racemes, and produced rather sparsely.

Nesæa (Lythrarieæ).

NESÆA SALICIFOLIA (*syn Heimia salicifolia*).—Mexico, 1821. This can only be styled as half-hardy, but with wall protection it forms a pretty bush often fully a yard in height. The leaves resemble those of some species of Willow, being long and narrow, while the showy yellow flowers are freely produced in August and September. It thrives best when planted in light, dry soil, and in a sheltered position.

Neviusa (Rosaceæ).

NEVIUSA ALABAMENSIS.—Alabama Snow Wreath. Alabama, 1879. This is a rare American shrub, with leaves reminding one of those of the Nine Bark, Neillia opulifolia, and the flowers, which are freely produced along the full length of the shoots, are white or yellowish-green, with prominent stamens of a tufted brush-like character. It is usually treated as a greenhouse plant, but may be seen growing and flowering freely in the open ground at Kew.

Notospartium (Leguminosæ).

NOTOSPARTIUM CARMICHÆLIÆ.—New Zealand. A curious shrub with slender, tortuous branches which are rounded and rush-like, and destitute of true leaves. The pinkish, pea-like flowers are freely produced, and the plant has succeeded and done well for many years back in some of the Royal parks. It thrives best in light, peaty soil, and where the drainage is good.

Nuttallia (Rosaceæ).

NUTTALLIA CERASIFORMIS.—Osoberry. California, 1848. This shrub is of great value on account of the flowers being produced in the early weeks of the year and when these are few and far between. It grows from 6 feet to 10 feet high, with a thick, twiggy head, and drooping racemes of white flowers borne thickly all over the plant. Few soils come amiss to this neglected shrub, it growing and flowering freely even on poor gravelly clay, and where only a limited number of shrubs could succeed.

Olearia (Compositæ).

Olearia Haastii.—New Zealand, 1872. This Composite shrub is only hardy in the milder parts of England and Ireland. It is of stiff, dwarf growth, rarely growing more than 4 feet high, but of neat and compact habit. Flowering as it does in late summer it is rendered of special value, the Daisy-like white blossoms being produced in large and flat clusters at the branch tips. The leaves are neat and of leathery texture, and being evergreen lend an additional charm to the shrub.

O. macrodonta (*syn O. dentata*), from New Zealand, 1886, is tolerably hardy, and may be seen in good form both at Kew and in the South of Ireland. The large Holly-like leaves are of a peculiar silvery-green tint above, and almost white on the undersides. Flowers white, and produced in dense heads in June and July. O. Forsterii (New Zealand, 1866) and O. Gunniana (*syn Eurybia Gunniana*) are nearly hardy species, the latter, from New Zealand, bearing a profusion of white Daisy-like flowers on dense, twiggy branches. They all thrive in good garden soil.

Ononis (Leguminosæ).

Ononis arvensis (*syn O. spinosa*).—Restharrow. A native undershrub of very variable size, according to the position in which it is found growing. It creeps along the ground, the shoots sending out roots as they proceed, and is usually found on dry sandy banks. The flowers when at their best are very ornamental, being bright pink, and with the standard streaked with a deeper shade. They are abundantly produced, and render the plant very conspicuous during the summer and autumn months. When planted on an old wall, and allowed to roam at will, the Restharrow is, perhaps, seen to best advantage.

O. ROTUNDIFOLIA.—South Europe, 1570. This is a very desirable half-shrubby species with trifoliate leaves and abundantly produced rosy flowers. The variety O. rotundifolia splendens is even better than the parent. Light, warm soil suits them best.

Ornus. See Fraxinus.

Osmanthus (Oleaceæ).

OSMANTHUS AQUIFOLIUM ILICIFOLIUS. — Holly-leaved Osmanthus. Japan. This is a handsome evergreen shrub, with Holly-like leaves, and not very conspicuous greenish-white flowers. It is a very desirable shrub, of which there are varieties named O. A. ilicifolius argenteo-variegatus, O. A. ilicifolius aureo-variegatus, and O. A. ilicifolius nanus, the names of which will be sufficient to define their characters.

O. A. ILICIFOLIUS MYRTIFOLIUS.—Myrtle-leaved Osmanthus. A very distinct and beautiful shrub, with unarmed leaves. It is of dwarf, compact growth, with small, sharply-pointed leaves and inconspicuous flowers. For the front line of a shrubbery this is an invaluable shrub, its pretty leaves and neat twiggy habit making it a favourite with planters. The variety rotundifolius is seldom seen in cultivation, but being distinct in foliage from any of the others is to be recommended. They grow freely in any good garden soil, but all the better if a little peat is added at the time of planting.

Ostrya (Cupuliferæ).

OSTRYA CARPINIFOLIA (*syn O. vulgaris*).—Common Hop Hornbeam. South Europe, 1724. A much-branched, round-headed tree, with cordate ovate, acuminate leaves. Both this and the following species, by reason of the resemblance between their female catkins and those of the Hop, and between their leaves and those of the Hornbeam, have acquired the very descriptive name of Hop Hornbeam. This is a large-growing tree, specimens in various parts of the country ranging in height from 50 feet to 60 feet. The flowers are greenish-white.

O. VIRGINICA.—Virginian Hop Hornbeam. Eastern United States, 1692. This resembles the latter, but is of smaller growth, rarely exceeding 40 feet in height. They grow fairly well in almost any class of soil, and on account of the long and showy catkins are well worthy of cultivation.

Oxycoccos (Vacciniaceæ).

OXYCOCCOS MACROCARPUS (*syn Vaccinium macrocarpum*).—North America, 1760. This is a creeping shrub with elliptic-oblong leaves and pinky flowers in spring. It is known as the American Cranberry, and is largely cultivated for its fruit.

O. PALUSTRIS (*syn Vaccinium Oxycoccos*) (Britain) has creeping, filiform stems, pink flowers, and dark-red berries that are strongly acid. Natives of damp, swampy ground.

Oxydendron (Ericaceæ).

OXYDENDRON ARBOREUM (*syn Andromeda arborea*).—Sorrel-tree. Eastern United States, 1752. Unfortunately this species is not often found under cultivation, being unsuitable generally for our climate. In some instances, however, it has done well, a specimen in the Knap Hill Nursery, Surrey, being 30 feet high, and with a dense rounded head. The flowers are very beautiful, being of a waxy white, and produced abundantly. It wants a free rich soil, and not too exposed site.

Ozothamnus (Compositæ).

OZOTHAMNUS ROSMARINIFOLIUS.—Australia, 1827. A pretty little Australian Composite, forming a dense, twiggy shrub, with narrow, Rosemary-like leaves, and small, whitish, Aster-like flowers which resemble those of its near relative, the Olearia, and are produced so thickly that the plant looks like a sheet of white when the blooms are fully developed. It flowers in June and July. In most parts of the country it will require protection, but can be classed as fairly hardy. Cuttings root freely if placed in sandy soil in a cool frame.

Pæonia (Pæonieæ).

PÆONIA MOUTAN.—Moutan Pæony, or Chinese Tree Pæony. China and Japan, 1789. A beautiful shrubby species introduced from China fully one hundred years ago. The first of the kind introduced to England had single flowers, and the plant is figured in Andrews' *Botanists' Repository* (tab. 463) under the name of P. papaveracea. The flowers are white with a dark-red centre. In the *Botanical Magazine* (tab. 2175), the same plant is figured under the name of P. Moutan var. papaveracea. This is perfectly hardy in our gardens, and is the parent of many beautiful and distinct varieties, including double and single white, pink, crimson, purple, and striped. It grows slowly in good garden soil.

Paliurus (Rhamnaceæ).

PALIURUS ACULEATUS (*syn P. australis*).—Christ's Thorn, or Garden Thorn. Mediterranean region, 1596. A densely-branched, spiny shrub, with small leaves and not very showy, yellowish-green flowers. It grows and flowers freely enough in light, peaty earth, but is not very hardy, the tips of the branches being usually killed back should the winter be at all severe.

Parrotia (Hamamelideæ).

PARROTIA PERSICA.—Persia, 1848. Well known for the lovely autumnal tints displayed by the foliage when dying off. But for the flowers, too, it is well worthy of culture, the crimson-tipped stamens of the male flowers being singularly beautiful and uncommon. In February it is no unusual sight to see on well-established plants whole branches that are profusely furnished with these showy flowers. For planting in a warm corner of a rather dry border it seems to be well suited; but it is perfectly hardy and free of growth when soil and site are agreeable. It is as yet rare in cultivation, but is sure, when better known and more widely disseminated, to become a general favourite with lovers of hardy shrubs.

Passiflora (Passifloreæ).

PASSIFLORA CÆRULEA.—Passion Flower. Brazil and Peru, 1699. Though not perfectly hardy, yet this handsome climbing plant, if cut down to the ground, usually shoots up freely again in the spring. The flowers, which are produced very freely, but particularly in maritime districts, vary from white to blue, and the prettily-fringed corona and centre of the flower render the whole peculiarly interesting and beautiful. P. cærulea Constance Elliott has greenish-white flowers; and P. cærulea Colvillei has white sepals and a blue fringe. The latter is of more robust growth, and more floriferous than the species. Turfy loam will suit their wants.

Paulownia (Scrophularineæ).

PAULOWNIA IMPERIALIS.—Japan, 1840. This is a handsome, fast-growing tree, and one that is particularly valuable for its ample foliage and distinct and showy flowers. Though perfectly hardy, in other respects it is unfortunate that the season at which the Paulownia flowers is so early that, unless the conditions are unusually favourable, the flower buds get destroyed by the frost. The tree grows to fully 40 feet high in this country, and is a grandly decorative object in its foliage alone, and for which, should the flowers never be produced, it is well worthy of cultivation. They are ovate-cordate, thickly covered with a greyish, woolly tomentum, and often measure, but particularly in young and healthy trees, as much as 10 inches in length. The Foxglove-like flowers are purplish-violet and spotted, and borne in terminal panicles. They are sweetly scented. When favourably situated, and in cool, sandy loam or peaty earth, the growth of the tree is very rapid, and when a tree has been cut over, the shoots sent out exceed 6 feet in length in one season, and nearly 2 inches in diameter. There are many fine old trees throughout the country which testify to the general hardihood of the Paulownia.

Pavia. See Æsculus.

Periploca (Asclepiadeæ).

PERIPLOCA GRÆCA.—Poison Vine. South-Eastern Europe, and Orient, 1597. A tall, climbing shrub, with small, ovate-lanceolate leaves and clusters of curious purplish-brown, green-tipped flowers produced in summer. The long, incurved appendages, in the shape of a crown, and placed so as to protect the style and anthers, render the flowers of peculiar interest. Though often used as a greenhouse plant, it is perfectly hardy, and makes a neat, deciduous wall or arch covering, thriving to perfection in rich soil that is well drained. It is readily propagated from cuttings.

Pernettya (Ericaceæ).

PERNETTYA MUCRONATA (*syn Arbutus mucronata*).—Prickly Heath. Magellan, 1828. This is a dwarf-growing, wiry shrub, with narrow, stiff leaves, and bears an abundance of white, bell-shaped flowers. It is a capital wind screen, and may be used to advantage on the exposed side of rock-work or flower beds, or as an ornamental shrub by the pond or lake side. The small dark-green leaves, the tiny white flowers, and great abundance of deep-purple berries in winter, are all points that are in favour of the shrub for extended cultivation. The pretty, pinky shoots, too, help to make the plant attractive even in mid-winter. Propagation by layers or seed is readily brought about. To grow this shrub to perfection, peaty soil or decayed vegetable matter will be found most suitable. There is a narrow-leaved form named P. mucronata angustfolia, and another on which the name of P. mucronata speciosa has been bestowed.

There are many beautiful-berried forms of the Pernettya, but as their flowers are small and inconspicuous, can hardly be included in our list.

Persica. See Prunus.

Philadelphus (Saxifrageæ).

PHILADELPHUS CORONARIUS.—Mock Orange, or Syringa. South Europe, 1596. A well-known and valuable garden shrub, of from 6 feet to 10 feet high, with ovate and serrulated leaves and pretty racemes of white or yellowish-white fragrant flowers in May. P. coronarius aureo-variegatus is one of the numerous forms of this shrub, having brightly-tinted, golden foliage, but the flowers are in no way superior to those of the parent. It is, if only for the foliage, an extremely pretty and distinct variety. P. coronarius argenteo-variegatus has silvery-tinted leaves; P. coronarius flore-pleno, full double flowers; and P. coronarius Keteleeri flore-pleno is the best double-flowered form in cultivation.

P. GORDONIANUS (*syn P. californicus*), an American species (1839), is a well-known and beautiful shrub, in which the flowers are usually double the size of those of the common species, and which are not produced till July, while those of P. coronarius appear in early May.

P. GRANDIFLORUS (*syns P. floribundus, P. latifolius,* and *P. speciosus*).—Southern United States, 1811. This has rotundate, irregularly-toothed leaves, and large white, sweetly-scented flowers produced in clusters. It forms a stout bush 10 feet high, and as much through. There are two varieties, P. grandiflorus laxus, a beautiful shrub, wreathed with large, pure white flowers, which are 2 inches across, and being loosely disposed, their individual beauty is greater than those of the type. They are also produced about ten days later. P. grandiflorus speciosissimus is another distinct and pretty kind.

P. HIRSUTUS.—North America, 1820. Another handsome, small-flowered species, of dwarf growth, and having hairy leaves. The white flowers are produced in threes.

P. INODORUS, also from North America (1738), differs little in size and shape of flowers from P. grandiflorus, but the flowers are without scent. The leaves, too, are quite glabrous and obscurely toothed.

P. Lemoinei Boule d'Argent is a cross, raised in 888, from P. Lemoinei and the double-flowered form of P. coronarius. The flowers are double white and with the pleasant, but not heavy, scent of P. microphyllus. P. Lemoinei Gerbe de Neige bears pleasantly-scented flowers that are as large as those of the well-known P. speciosissimus; while Candelabre and Manteu D'hermine are other desirable kinds. There is an erect form of P. Lemoinei named erectus that is also worthy of note.

P. Lewisi, from North America (1839), is hardly sufficiently distinct from some of the others to warrant special notice. The flowers are small and arranged in threes.

P. microphyllus, from New Mexico (1883), is of low growth, and remarkable for its slender branches, small, Myrtle-like leaves, and abundance of small white flowers. It is a decidedly pretty shrub, but is not so hardy as the others. P. microphyllus erectus is of upright habit.

P. satzumi (*syn P. chinensis*).—Japan, 1851. A slender-growing species, with long and narrow leaves and large white flowers produced in pairs.

P. tomentosus (India, 1822) and P. mexicanus (Mexico, 1839) are other species that might be worthy of including in a representative collection of these plants.

This is a valuable genus of shrubs, all being remarkable for the abundance of white, and usually sweet-scented, flowers which they produce. They require no special treatment, few soils, if at all free and rich, coming amiss to them; while even as shrubs for shady situations they are not to be despised. Propagation is effected by means of cuttings, which root freely if placed in sandy soil.

Phillyrea (Oleaceæ).

P. ANGUSTIFOLIA (narrow-leaved Phillyrea), P. ilicifolia (Holly-leaved Phillyrea), P. salicifolia (Willow-leaved Phillyrea), P. buxifolia (Box-leaved Phillyrea), and P. ligustrifolia (Privet-leaved Phillyrea), are all more or less valuable species, and their names indicate their peculiarities of leafage. P. angustifolia rosmarinifolia (*syn P. neapolitana*) is a somewhat rare shrub, but one that is well worthy of culture, if only for its neat habit and tiny little Rosemary-like leaves. It is from Italy, and known under the synonym of *P. rosmarinifolia*.

P. LATIFOLIA (*syn P. obliqua*).—Broad-leaved Phillyrea. South Europe, 1597. This is a compact-growing and exceedingly ornamental shrub, with bright and shining ovate-serrulated leaves. For its handsome, evergreen foliage and compact habit of growth it is, perhaps, most to be valued, for the small flowers are, at their best, both dull and inconspicuous. Not very hardy unless in the sea-coast garden.

P. MEDIA (*syns P. ligustrifolia* and *P. oleæfolia*).—South Europe, 1597. This is another interesting species, but not at all common in cultivation. The white flowers are produced in May.

P. VILMORINIANA (*syns P. laurifolia* and *P. decora*).—Asia Minor, 1885. This is a grand addition to these valuable shrubs, of which it is decidedly the best from an ornamental point of view. It is of compact growth, with large, Laurel-like leaves, which are of a pleasing shade of green, fully 4 inches long, and of stout, leathery texture; while the racemes of white flowers are freely produced. That this shrub is perfectly hardy is now a well-established fact.

The Phillyreas succeed well in light, warm, but not too dry soil, and they do all the better if a warm and sheltered position is assigned to them, while for town planting they are valuable. Being unusually bright of foliage they are of great service in planting for shrubbery embellishment, which they light up in a very conspicuous manner during the dull winter months. They get shabby and meagre foliaged if exposed to cold winds.

Phlomis (Labiatæ).

PHLOMIS FRUTICOSA.—Jerusalem Sage. Mediterranean region, 1596. This is a neat-growing, shrubby plant, with ovate acute leaves that are covered with a yellowish down. From the axils of the upper leaves the whorls of showy yellow flowers are freely produced during the summer months. It is valued for its neat growth, and as growing on dry soils where few other plants could eke out an existence.

Photinia (Rosaceæ).

PHOTINIA ARBUTIFOLIA (*syns Cratægus arbutifolia* and *Mespilus arbutifolia*).—Arbutus-leaved Photinia, or Californian May-bush. California, 1796. This is a very distinct shrub, with bright-red bark on the young wood, and leaves resembling those of the Strawberry Tree (Arbutus), the white flowers being in an elongated panicle.

P. BENTHAMIANA is only worthy of culture for its neat habit and freedom of growth when suitably placed.

P. JAPONICA (*syn Eriobotrya japonica*). Loquat, Japan Medlar, or Japan Quince. Japan, 1787. This is chiefly remarkable for its handsome foliage, the leaves being oblong in shape and downy on the undersides. The white flowers are of no great beauty, but being produced at the beginning of winter, and when flowers are scarce, are all the more welcome, while the orange-red fruit is about the size of a small apple. It requires protection in all but the warmer parts of these islands, and does well in any good garden soil.

P. SERRULATA (*syn Cratægus glabra*).—Chinese Hawthorn. Japan and China, 1804. This has Laurel-like leaves, 4 inches or 5 inches long, and, especially when young, of a beautiful rosy-chocolate colour, and clustered at the branch tips. Flowers small, white, and produced in flat corymbs. An invaluable seaside shrub.

They all grow well either in light, rich loam, or in sandy, peaty earth, and are usually propagated by grafting.

Phyllodoce (Ericaceæ).

PHYLLODOCE TAXIFOLIA (*syns P. cærulea* and *Menziesia cærulea*).—An almost extinct native species, having crowded linear leaves, and lilac-blue flowers. It is only of value for rock gardening. For P. empetriformis, see Bryanthus.

Pieris (Ericaceæ).

PIERIS FLORIBUNDA (*syns Andromeda floribunda* and *Leucothoë floribunda*).—United States, 1812. Few perfectly hardy shrubs are more beautiful than this, with its pure-white, Lily-of-the-Valley-like flowers, borne in dense racemes, and small, neat, dark-green leaves. To cultivate this handsome shrub in a satisfactory way, fairly rich loam or peat and a situation sheltered from cold and cutting winds are necessities.

P. FORMOSA (1880) is not very hardy, but is a beautiful evergreen shrub, with coriaceous, finely serrated leaves and porcelain-white flowers in branching clusters.

P. JAPONICA (*syn Andromeda japonica*).—Japan, 1882. A hardy, well-known shrub, that was first brought specially under notice in *The Garden*, in which a coloured plate and description were given. It is thickly furnished with neat and small deep-green, leathery leaves, and pretty, waxy-white flowers, pendulous at the branch tips. Planted in free, sandy peat, it thrives vigorously, and soon forms a neat specimen of nearly a yard in height. It is a very desirable hardy species, and one that can be confidently recommended for ornamental planting. There is a variegated variety, P. japonica elegantissima, with leaves clearly edged with creamy-white and flushed with pink. Amongst variegated, small-growing shrubs it is a gem.

P. MARIANA (*syn Andromeda Mariana ovalis*).—North America, 1736. A neat shrub about 3 feet in height, with oval leaves, and pretty white flowers in pendent clusters produced in May and June.

P. OVALIFOLIA (*syn Andromeda ovalifolia*).—Nepaul, 1825. A fine, tall-growing species, with oval-pointed, leathery leaves placed on long footstalks. Flowers in lengthened, drooping, one-sided racemes, and white or pale-flesh coloured. Being perfectly hardy, and attaining to as much as 20 feet in height, it is a desirable species for the lawn or shrubbery.

P. PHILLYREÆFOLIA (Florida, 1842) produces its white flowers from January onwards, but is not very hardy.

Piptanthus (Leguminosæ).

PIPTANTHUS NEPALENSIS (*syn Baptisia nepalensis* and *Thermopsis laburnifolia*).—Evergreen Laburnum. Temperate Himalaya, 1821. A handsome, half-hardy shrub, of often fully 10 feet high, with trifoliate, evergreen leaves, and terminal racemes of large yellow flowers. In the South and West of England and Ireland it does well, and only receives injury during very severe winters. Planted either as a single specimen, or in clumps of three or five, the evergreen Laburnum has a pleasing effect, whether with its bright, glossy-green leaves, or abundance of showy flowers. It is of somewhat erect growth, with stout branches and plenty of shoots. Propagated from seed, which it ripens abundantly in this country.

P. NEPALENSIS AUREA (1879) has the bark striped yellow and green.

Pittosporum (Pittosporeæ).

PITTOSPORUM TOBIRA.—Japan, 1804. This forms a neat, evergreen shrub, with deep-green, leathery leaves, and clusters of white, fragrant flowers, each about an inch in diameter. It is hardy in the more favoured parts of the South and West of England, where it makes a reliable seaside shrub.

P. UNDULATUM, from Australia (1789), is also hardy against a wall, but cannot be depended upon generally. It is a neat shrub, with waxy leaves that are rendered conspicuous by the dark midribs and white flowers. They grow well in any good garden soil.

Plagianthus (Malvaceæ).

PLAGIANTHUS LAMPENII.—Van Dieman's Land, 1833. This is about equally hardy with P. Lyalli, and produces a great abundance of sweetly-scented pale-yellow flowers.

P. LYALLI, a native of New Zealand (1871), and a member of the Mallow family, is a free-flowering and beautiful shrub, but one that cannot be recommended for general planting in this country. At Kew it does well and flowers freely on an east wall. The flowers are snow-white, with golden-yellow anthers, and produced on the ends of the last season's branchlets during June and July. The flower-stalks, being fully 2 inches long, give to the flowers a very graceful appearance. In this country the leaves are frequently retained till spring.

P. PULCHELLUS (*syn Sida pulchella*).—Australia and

Tasmania. Another half-hardy species, which bears, even in a young state, an abundance of rather small whitish flowers. Light, rich soil should be used in their culture.

Planera. See Zelkova.

Polycarpa. See Idesia.

Polygala (Polygaleæ).

POLYGALA CHAMÆBUXUS.—Bastard Box. A neat little shrubby plant, about 6 inches high, with small ovate, coriaceous leaves and fragrant yellow and cream flowers. P. chamæbuxus purpureus differs in bearing rich reddish-purple flowers, and is one of the most showy and beautiful of rock plants. They are natives of Europe (1658), and grow best in vegetable mould.

Polygonum (Polygonaceæ).

POLYGONUM BALDSCHUANICUM.—Bokhara, 1888. A beautiful climber that grows to nearly 20 feet in height, with ovate, heart-shaped leaves and long terminal panicles of pinkish-white flowers. It is of rapid growth, with twining stems, and succeeds well in light loamy soil and in full sunshine. For covering a pergola, old tree stump, or unhealthy, thin-foliaged tree, it has, perhaps, no equal amongst hardy climbers.

P. MULTIFLORUM.—Japan and China, 1881. This grows to 20 feet in height in one season, the stems being slender, and reddish in colour, while the spreading panicles of whitish flowers are produced in abundance.

P. VACCINIFOLIUM.—Himalaya, 1845. This is a sub-shrubby species, with small, oblong-ovate, acute-pointed leaves and terminal spikes of bright rosy-red flowers produced freely towards the end of summer. It is of creeping habit, rarely rising more than a few inches from the ground. Sandy loam or peat will suit it well.

The commonly cultivated species, P. SACHALINENSE, with large foliage and racemes of yellowish-white flowers, is only of perennial growth. They succeed best in rich, dampish loam.

Potentilla (Rosaceæ).

POTENTILLA FRUTICOSA.—Northern Hemisphere (Britain). An indigenous shrub that grows about a yard high, with pinnate leaves and golden flowers. It is a most persistent blooming plant, as often for four months, beginning in June, the flowers are produced freely in succession. It delights to grow in a strong soil, and, being of low, sturdy growth, does well for the outer line of the shrubbery.

Prinos (Ilicineæ).

PRINOS GLABER (*syn Ilex glabra*).—North America, 1759. (Ink-berry.) This is a pretty evergreen shrub about a yard high, with dark glossy leaves and small white flowers mostly produced in threes during July and August. The berries are jet black, and in consequence of their colour are called ink-berries. It succeeds best in sandy loam and peat.

Prunopsis, See Prunus.

Prunus (Rosaceæ). Including Amygdalus, Amygdalopsis, Cerasus, Prunopsis, and Persica.

PRUNUS AMERICANA (*syn P. nigra*).—This grows to 20 feet high with ovate or obovate, pointed, serrated leaves, and white flowers in April. Fruit yellow or red, and about three-fourths of an inch in diameter.

P. AMYGDALUS (*syn Amygdalus communis*).—Common

Almond. Barbary, 1548. Whether by a suburban roadside, or even in the heart of the crowded city, the Almond seems quite at home, and is at once one of the loveliest and most welcome of early spring-flowering trees. The flowers are rather small for the family, pale pink, and produced in great quantity before the leaves. There are several distinct forms of the Almond, differing mainly in the colour of the flowers, one being pink, another red, while a third has double flowers. P. Amygdalus macrocarpa (Large-fruited Almond) is by far the handsomest variety in cultivation, the flowers being large, often 3 inches in diameter, and white tinged with pink, particularly at the base of the petals. The flowers, too, are produced earlier than those of any other Almond, while the tree is of stout growth and readily suited with both soil and site.

P. Amygdalus dulcis (*syn A. dulcis*).—Sweet Almond, of which there are three distinct varieties, P. A. dulcis purpurea, P. A. dulcis macrocarpa, and P. A. dulcis pendula, should be included in every collection of these handsome flowering plants.

P. Avium Juliana (*syn Cerasus Juliana*).—St. Julian's Cherry. South Europe. This bears large flowers of a most beautiful and delicate blush tint. P. Avium multiplex is a double form of the Wild Cherry, or Gean, with smaller leaves than the type.

P. Boissierii (*syn Amygdalus Boissierii*).—Asia Minor, 1879. This is a bushy shrub, with almost erect, long, and slender branches, and furnished with leaves an inch in length, elliptic, and thick of texture. Flowers pale flesh-coloured, and produced abundantly. It is a very ornamental and distinct plant, and is sure, when better known, to attract a considerable amount of attention.

P. cerasifera (*syn P. Myrobalana*).—Cherry, or Myrobalan Plum. Native Country unknown. A medium-sized tree, with an abundance of small white flowers, which are particularly attractive if they escape the early spring frosts. It is of stout, branching habit, with a well-rounded head, and has of late years attracted a good deal of notice as a hedge plant. P. cerasifera Pissardii, the purple-leaved Cherry plum, is a remarkable and handsome variety, in which the leaves are deep purple, thus rendering the plant one of the most distinct and ornamental-foliaged of the family. It produces its white, blush-tinted flowers in May. It was received by M. A. Chatenay, of Sceau, from M. Pissard, director of the garden of His Majesty the Shah of Persia. When it flowered it was figured in the *Revue Horticole*, 1881, p. 190.

P. CERASUS (*syn Cerasus vulgaris*).—Common Cherry. A favourite medium-sized tree, and one that lends itself readily to cultivation. As an ornamental park tree this Cherry, though common, must not be despised, for during summer, when laden with its pure-white flowers, or again in autumn when myriads of the black, shining fruits hang in clusters from its branches, it will be readily admitted that few trees have a more beautiful or conspicuous appearance, P. Cerasus flore-pleno (double-flowered Cherry) is a distinct and desirable variety. P. Cerasus multiplex is a very showy double form, more ornamental than P. Avium multiplex, and also known under the names of *Cerasus ranunculiflora* and *C. Caproniana multiplex*. P. Cerasus semperflorens (*syn Cerasus semperflorens*), the All Saints, Ever Flowering, or Weeping, Cherry, is another valuable variety, of low growth, and with gracefully drooping branches, particularly when the tree is old. It is a very desirable lawn tree, and flowers at intervals during the summer.

P. CHAMÆCERASUS (*syn Cerasus Chamæcerasus*).—Ground Cherry. Europe, 1597. This is a dwarf, slender-branched, and gracefully pendent shrub, of free growth, undoubted hardihood, and well worthy of extended cultivation. The variety C. Chamæcerasus variegata has the leaves suffused with greenish-lemon. There is also a creeping form named P. Chamæcerasus pendula.

P. Davidiana (*syn Persica*).—Abbé David's Almond. China. This is the tree to which, under the name of Amygdalus Davidiana alba, a First-class Certificate was awarded in 1892 by the Royal Horticultural Society. The typical species is a native of China, from whence it was introduced several years ago, but it is still far from common. It is the earliest of the Almonds to unfold its white flowers, for in mild winters some of them expand before the end of January; but March, about the first week, it is at its best. It is of more slender growth than the common Almond, and the flowers, which are individually smaller, are borne in great profusion along the shoots of the preceding year, so that a specimen, when in full flower, is quite one mass of bloom. There is a rosy-tinted form known as Amygdalus Davidiana rubra.

P. divaricata, from the Caucasus (1822), is useful on account of the pure-white flowers being produced early in the year, and before the leaves. It has a graceful, easy habit of growth, and inclined to spread, and makes a neat lawn or park specimen.

P. domestica, Common Garden Plum, and P. domestica insititia, Bullace Plum, are both very ornamental flowering species, and some of the varieties are even more desirable than the parent plants.

P. ilicifolia (*syn Cerasus ilicifolius*).—Holly-leaved Cherry. California. A distinct evergreen species, with thick leathery leaves, and erect racemes of small white flowers. A native of dry hilly ground along the coast from San Francisco to San Diego. Hardy in most situations, but requiring light warm soil and a dry situation.

P. Jackuemontii.—Himalayas, 1866. This is a rare, hardy shrub, about 10 feet high, with nearly obovate leaves, and pinky flowers produced in May.

P. LAUNESIANA (*syn Cerasus Launesiana*).—Japan, 1870. This is a valuable addition to the already long list of ornamental flowering Cherries. It flowers in the early spring, when the tree is literally enshrouded in rose-coloured flowers, and which produce a very striking effect. The tree is quite hardy, flowers well even in a young state, and will grow in any soil that suits our common wild species.

P. LAUROCERASUS (*syn Cerasus Laurocerasus*).—Common, or Cherry Laurel. Levant, 1629. Although a well-known garden and park shrub, of which a description is unnecessary, the common or Cherry Laurel, when in full flower, must be ranked amongst our more ornamental shrubs. There are several varieties all worthy of culture for the sake of their evergreen leaves and showy flower spikes. P. Laurocerasus rotundifolia has leaves that are broader in proportion to their length than those of the common species; P. Laurocerasus caucasica is of sturdy growth, with deep-green leaves, and a compact habit of growth; P. Laurocerasus colchica is the freest-flowering Laurel in cultivation, with horizontally arranged branches and pale-green leaves; P. Laurocerasus latifolia, a rather tender shrub, with bold handsome foliage; and P. Laurocerasus parvifolia, of low growth, but never very satisfactory in appearance. Three other less common forms might also be mentioned: P. Laurocerasus angustifolia, with narrow leaves; P. Laurocerasus camelliæfolia, with thick leathery foliage; and P. Laurocerasus intermedia, halfway between P. Laurocerasus angustifolia and the common Laurel.

P. LUSITANICA (*syn Cerasus lusitanica*).—Portugal Laurel. Portugal, 1648. A well-known shrub or small-growing tree, and one of the most valuable of all our hardy evergreens. It is of neat and compact growth, with a good supply of bright-green shining foliage, and bears long spikes of pleasing creamy-white perfumed flowers. P.

lusitanica myrtifolia (Myrtle-leaved Portugal Laurel) differs from the species in the smaller, longer, and narrower leaves, which are more thickly arranged, and in its more decided upright habit of growth. P. lusitanica variegata is hardly sufficiently constant or distinct to warrant recommendation. P. lusitanica azorica, from the Azores, is of more robust growth than the common plant, with larger and richer green leaves, and the bark of the younger branches is of a very decided reddish tinge.

P. MAHALEB (*syn Cerasus Mahaleb*).—The Mahaleb, or Perfumed Cherry. South Europe, 1714. This and its variegated variety, P. Mahaleb variegata, are very free-flowering shrubs, and of neat growth. The variegated variety is well worthy of attention, having a clear silvery variegation, chiefly confined to the leaf margin, but in a less degree to the whole of the foliage, and imparting to it a bright, glaucous tint that is highly ornamental. There is a partially weeping form named P. Mahaleb pendula.

P. MARITIMA.—Beach, or Sand Plum. North America, 1800. A prostrate, spreading shrub, that is of value for planting in poor sandy soil, and along the sea-coast. The flowers are small, but plentifully produced. There is a form named P. pygmæa.

P. NANA (*syns Amygdalus nana* and *A. Besseriana*).—Dwarf Almond. From Tartary, 1683. This is of dwarf, twiggy growth, rarely more than 3 feet high, and bearing an abundance of rose-coloured flowers in early February. From its neat, small growth, and rich profusion of flowers, this dwarf Almond may be reckoned as a most useful and desirable shrub. Suckers are freely produced in any light free soil.

P. PADUS (*syn Cerasus Padus*).—Bird Cherry or Hagberry. An indigenous species, with oblong, doubly-serrated leaves, and terminal or axillary racemes of pure-white flowers. It is a handsome and distinct small-growing tree, and bears exposure at high altitudes in a commendable manner.

P. PANICULATA FLORE-PLENO (*syns Cerasus serrulata flore-pleno* and *C. Sieboldii*).—China, 1822. This is one of the most desirable of the small-growing and double-flowered Cherries. It is of neat growth, with short, stout branches that are sparsely furnished with twigs, and smooth, obovate, pointed leaves, bristly serrated on the margins. Flowers double and white at first, but afterwards tinged with pink, freely produced and of good, lasting substance. P. paniculata Watereri is a handsome variety that most probably may be linked to the species.

P. PENNSYLVANICA.—American Wild Red Cherry. North America, 1773. This is an old-fashioned garden tree, and one of the choicest, producing in May a great abundance of its tiny white flowers.

P. PERSICA (*syns Amygdalus Persica* and *Persica vulgaris*), common Peach, is likewise well worthy of culture, there being white, rose, and crimson-flowering forms. P. Persica lævis (the Nectarine), 1562, has red flowers and smooth fruit. The beautiful P. Persica magnifica, from Japan, is a semi-double form, with brilliant crimson flowers, which are produced in early spring.

P. PUDDUM (*syns P. Pseudo-cerasus* and *Cerasus Pseudo-cerasus*).—Bastard Cherry. China, 1891. There are very few more ornamental trees in cultivation in this country than the double-flowered Cherry. It makes a charming small-growing tree, is of free growth and perfectly hardy, and one of, if not the most, floriferous of the tribe. The flowers are individually large, pinky or purplish-white, and produced with the leaves in April. The variety James H. Veitch has deep rose-pink double flowers in early spring, and is a very ornamental form.

P. SINENSIS.—China, 1869. A Chinese Plum of somewhat slender growth, and with the branches wreathed in small white flowers. It is often seen as a pot plant, but it is one of the hardiest of its family. P. sinensis flore-pleno is a double white form, and the most ornamental for pot work. There is also a variety with rose-col red flowers.

P. SPINOSA.—Sloe, or Blackthorn. An indigenous, spiny shrub, with tiny white flowers; and P. spinosa flore-pleno has small, rosette-like flowers that are both showy and effective.

P. TOMENTOSA.—Japan, 1872. This is one of the most desirable of hardy shrubs, with large white, flesh-tinted flowers produced in the first weeks of March, and in such quantities as almost to hide the branches from view. It forms a well-rounded, dense bush of 5 feet or 6 feet high.

P. TRILOBA (*syns P. virgata, Amygdalopsis Lindleyi*, and *Prunopsis Lindleyi*).—China, 1857. This is a very handsome early-flowering shrub, that is at once recognized by the generally three-lobed leaves. It is one of the first to flower, the blossoms being produced in March and April, and sometimes even earlier when the plant is grown against a sunny, sheltered wall. The semi-double flowers are large and of good substance, and of a rosy-white tint, but deep rose in the bud state. There is a nursery form of this plant with white flowers, named P. triloba alba. It is quite hardy, bears pruning well, and grows quickly, soon covering a large space of a wall or warm, sunny bank. As an ornamental, flowering lawn shrub it has few equals, the blossoms remaining good for fully a fortnight.

P. VIRGINIANA (*syn Cerasus virginiana*) and P. SEROTINA (North America Bird Cherries) are worthy species, with long clusters of flowers resembling those of our native Bird Cherry. They are large-growing species, and, particularly the latter, are finding favour with cultivators in this country on account of their bold and ornamental appearance. They are all readily cultivated in any light, rich soil.

Ptelea (Rutaceæ).

Ptelea trifoliata.—Hop Tree, or Swamp Dogwood. North America, 1704. A small-growing tree, with trifoliate, yellowish-green leaves placed on long footstalks, and inconspicuous greenish flowers. The leaves, when bruised, emit an odour resembling Hops. P. trifoliata variegata is one of the handsomest of golden-leaved trees, and is well worthy of extensive planting. It is preferable in leaf colouring to the golden Elder. Perfectly hardy.

Pterostyrax. See Halesia.

Punica (Lythrarieæ).

Punica Granatum. — Pomegranate. For planting against a southern-facing wall this pretty shrub is well suited, but it is not sufficiently hardy for the colder parts of the country. Frequently in the more favoured parts of England and Ireland it reaches a height of 14 feet, with a branch-spread of nearly as much, and is then, when in full flower, an object of general admiration and of the greatest beauty. The flowers are of a rich, bright-scarlet colour, and well set off by the glossy, dark-green leaves. P. Granatum rubra flore-pleno is a decidedly ornamental shrub, in which the flowers are of a bright scarlet and perfectly double. They grow satisfactorily in light, but rich, soil.

Pyrus (Rosaceæ).

Pyrus alnifolia.—Japan, 1892. This has ovate, doubly serrated leaves, like those of the Alder, 2 inches or 3 inches long, and corymbs of not very attractive flowers.

P. AMERICANA (*syn Sorbus americana*).—American Mountain Ash. This species, a native of the mountains of Pennsylvania and Virginia (1782), is much like our Rowan Tree in general appearance, but the bunches of berries are larger, and of a brighter red colour.

P. ANGUSTIFOLIA.—North America, 1750. A double-flowered crab is offered under this name, of vigorous growth, bearing delicate pink, rose-like flowers that are deliciously fragrant, and borne contemporaneously with the leaves. The merits claimed for the shrub are perfect hardihood, great beauty of blossom and leaf, delicious fragrance, and adaptability to various soils. The single-flowered form extends over large areas in the Atlantic States of North America. They are very desirable, small-growing trees, and are described by Professor Sargent as being not surpassed in beauty by any of the small trees of North America.

P. ARIA.—White Beam Tree. Europe (Britain) A shrub or small-growing tree, with lobed leaves, covered thickly on the undersides with a close, flocculent down. The flowers are small and white, and produced in loose corymbs. It is a handsome small tree, especially when the leaves are ruffled by the wind and the undersides revealed to view. The red or scarlet fruit is showy and beautiful.

P. AUCUPARIA.—Mountain Ash, or Rowan Tree. Too well-known to need description, but one of our handsomest small-growing trees, and whether for the sake of its dense corymbs of small white flowers or large bunches of scarlet fruit it is always welcomed and admired. P. Aucuparia pendula has the branches inclined to be pendulous; and P. Aucuparia fructo-luteo differs from the normal plant in having yellowish instead of scarlet fruit.

P. BACCATA.—Siberian Crab. Siberia and Dahuria, 1784. This is one of the most variable species in cultivation, and from which innumerable forms have been developed, that differ either in habit, foliage, flowers, or fruit. The deciduous calyx would seem to be the only reliable distinguishing character. It is a widely-distributed species, being found in North China and Japan, Siberia, and the Himalayas, and has from time immemorial been cultivated by the Chinese and Japanese, so that it is not at all surprising that numbers of forms have been developed.

P. CARDINALIS (1893) is a desirable garden form, with conspicuous cardinal-red flowers, which are freely produced. It is a good town shrub.

P. CORONARIA.—Sweet Scented Crab. North America, 1724. This is a handsome species, with ovate, irregularly-toothed leaves and pink and white fragrant flowers. The flowers are individually large and corymbose, and are succeeded by small green fruit. P. Coronaria flore-pleno is a semi-double variety, that far surpasses the parent in point of beauty. The flowers are reddish-white, half an inch in diameter, and violet-scented.

P. DOMESTICA (*syn Sorbus domestica*).—True Service. Britain. This resembles the Mountain Ash somewhat, but the flowers are panicled, and the berries fewer, larger, and pear-shaped. The flowers are conspicuous enough to render the tree of value in ornamental planting.

P. FLORIBUNDA (*syns P. Malus floribunda* and *Malus microcarpa floribunda*).—China and Japan, 1818. The Japanese Crabs are wonderfully floriferous, the branches being in most instances wreathed with flowers that are individually not very large, and rarely exceeding an inch in diameter when fully expanded. Generally in the bud state the flowers are of a deep crimson, but this disappears as they become perfectly developed, and when a less striking tint of pinky-white is assumed. From the St. Petersburg gardens many very ornamental Crabs have been sent out, these differing considerably in colour of bark, habit, and tint of flowers. They have all been referred to the above species. P. floribunda is a worthy form, and one of the most brilliant of spring-flowering trees. The long, slender shoots are thickly covered for almost their entire length with flowers that are rich crimson in the bud state, but paler when fully opened. There are numerous, very distinct varieties, such as P. floribunda atrosanguinea, with deep-red flowers; P. floribunda Elise Rathe, of pendulous habit; P. floribunda John Downie, very beautiful in fruit; P. floribunda pendula, a semi-weeping variety; P. floribunda præcox, early-flowering; P. floribunda mitis, of small size; P. floribunda Helleana or Parkmanii, probably the most beautiful of all the forms; and P. floribunda Fairy Apple and P. floribunda Transcendant Crab, of interest on account of their showy fruit. P. floribunda Toringo (Toringo Crab) is a Japanese tree of small growth, with sharply-cut, usually three-lobed, pubescent leaves and small flowers. Fruit small, with deciduous calyx lobes.

P. GERMANICA (*syn Mespilus germanica*).—Common Medlar. Europe (Britain). Asia Minor, Persia. Early records show that the Medlar was cultivated for its fruit as early as 1596. Some varieties are still grown for that purpose, and in that state the tree is not devoid of ornament. The large white flowers are produced singly, but have a fine effect in their setting of long, lanceolate, finely-serrate leaves during May.

P. JAPONICA (*syn Cydonia japonica*).—Japanese Quince. Japan, 1815. This is one of the commonest of garden shrubs, and one that is peculiarly well suited for our climate, whether planted as a standard or as a wall plant. The flowers are brilliant crimson, and plentifully produced towards the end of winter and before the leaves. Besides the species there are several very fine varieties, including P. japonica albo cincta, P. japonica atropurpurea,

P. japonica coccinea, P. japonica flore-pleno, P. japonica nivalis, a charming species, with snowy-white flowers; P. japonica rosea, of a delicate rose-pink; and P. japonica princeps. P. japonica cardinalis is one of the best of the numerous forms of this beautiful shrub. The flowers are of large size, of full rounded form, and of a deep cardinal-rose colour. They are produced in great quantity along the branches. A well-grown specimen is in April a brilliant picture of vivid colour, and the shrub is sooner or later destined to a chief place amongst our ornamental flowering shrubs.

P. Maulei (*syn Cydonia Maulei*), Japan, 1874, has bright-red, freely-produced flowers, which are succeeded by golden-yellow fruit. It is one of the most ornamental of garden shrubs.

P. prunifolia.—Siberia, 1758. Whether in flower or fruit this beautiful species is sure to attract attention. It is a tree of 25 feet in height, with nearly rotundate, glabrous leaves on long footstalks, and pretty pinky-white flowers. The fruit is very ornamental, being, when fully ripe, of a deep and glowing scarlet, but there are forms with yellow and green, as also striped fruit.

P. rivularis.—River-side Wild Service Tree. North-West America, 1836. A native of North America, with terminal clusters of white flowers, succeeded by sub-globose red or yellow fruit, is an attractive and handsome species. The fruit is eaten by the Indians of the North-West, and the wood, which is very hard, and susceptible of a fine polish, is largely used in the making of wedges. It is a rare species in this country.

P. sinensis (*syn Cydonia chinensis*).—Chinese Quince. China, 1818. This is rarely seen in cultivation, it having, comparatively speaking, few special merits of recommendation.

P. sinica (*syn P. sinensis of Lindley*).—Chinese Pear Tree. China and Cochin China, 1820. Another very ornamental Crab, bearing a great abundance of rosy-pink or nearly white flowers. It is a shrub-like tree, reaching a height of 20 feet, and with an upright habit of growth. Bark of a rich, reddish-brown colour. It is one of the most profuse and persistent bloomers of the whole family.

P. SMITHII (*syn Mespilus Smithii* and *M. grandiflora*).—Smith's Medlar. Caucasus, 1800. The habit of this tree closely resembles that of a Hawthorn, and although the flowers are only half the size of those of the Common Medlar, they are produced in greater profusion, so that the round-headed tree becomes a sheet of white blossom during May and June. The reddish-brown fruits are small for a Medlar, and ripen in October.

P. TORMINALIS.—Wild Service Tree. A native species of small growth, with ovate-cordate leaves, and small white flowers. P. torminalis pinnatifida, with acutely-lobed leaves, and oval-oblong fruit may just be mentioned.

P. VESTITA.—Nepaul White Beam. Nepaul, 1820. In this species the leaves are very large, ovate-acute or elliptic, and when young thickly coated with a white woolly-like substance, but which with warm weather gradually gives way until they are of a smooth and shining green. The flowers are borne in woolly racemose corymbs, and are white succeeded by greenish-brown berries as large as marbles. It is of pyramidal growth, and attains to less than 20 feet in height.

Other species of less interest are P. varidosa, P. salicifolia, P. salvæfolia, P. Bollwylleriana, and P. Amygdaliformis. They are all of free growth, and the readiest culture, even in smoky localities, and being perfectly hardy are well worthy of a much larger share of attention than they have heretofore received.

Raphiolepis (Rosaceæ).

RAPHIOLEPIS JAPONICA INTEGERRIMA (*syn R. ovata*).—A Japanese shrub (1865), with deep-green, ovate, leathery leaves that are not over abundant, and produced generally at the branch tips. The pure-white or pinkish-white, fragrant flowers are plentifully produced when the plant is grown in a cosy corner, or on a sunny wall. Though seldom killed outright, the Raphiolepis becomes badly crippled in severe winters. It is, however, a bold and handsome shrub, and one that may be seen doing well in many gardens around London. There is a variegated variety. Loam and peat suits its wants in the matter of soil.

Rhamnus (Rhamneæ).

RHAMNUS ALATERNUS.—Mediterranean region, 1629. This is an evergreen shrub, with lanceolate shining leaves of a dark glossy-green colour, and pretty greenish flowers produced from March till June. There are several well-marked varieties, one with golden and another with silvery leaves, and named respectively, R. Alaternus foliis aurea and R. Alaternus foliis argenteus.

R. ALNIFOLIA.—North America, 1788. This grows about a yard high, with ovate serrated leaves 2 inches to 3 inches long, and greenish flowers produced in May and June.

R. ALPINUS.—Europe, 1752. This is a neat-growing species, with greenish flowers and black fruit.

R. CATHARTICUS.—Common Buckthorn, is a native, thorny species, with ovate, stalked leaves, and small, thickly-clustered greenish flowers, succeeded by black berries about the size of peas.

R. FRANGULA.—The Berry-bearing Alder. Europe and Britain. A more erect shrub than the former, and destitute of spines. The leaves, too, are larger, and the fruit of a dark-purple colour when ripe. More common in Britain than the R. catharticus.

Rhaphithamnus (Verbenaceæ).

RHAPHITHAMNUS CYANOCYRPUS (*syn Citharexylum cyanocarpum*).—Chili. This bears a great resemblance to some of the thorny Berberis, and is at once a distinct and beautiful shrub. The flowers are large and conspicuous, and of a taking bluish-lilac colour. Having stood unharmed in Ireland through the unusually severe winters of 1879–80, when many more common shrubs were killed outright, it may be relied upon as at least fairly hardy. The soil in which this rare and pretty shrub does best is a brown, fibrous peat, intermingled with sharp sand.

Rhododendron (Ericaceæ).

RHODODENDRON ARBORESCENS (*syn Azalea arborescens*), from the Carolina Mountains (1818), is a very showy, late-blooming species. The white, fragrant flowers and noble port, together with its undoubted hardihood, should make this shrub a general favourite with cultivators.

R. BRACHYCARPUM.—Japan, 1888. A robust, wide-spreading shrub, with pale-yellow or cream-coloured flowers which are dotted with green at the base of the petals.

R. CALENDULACEUM (*syn Azalea calendulacea*), from North America (1806), is another of the deciduous species, having oblong, hairy leaves and large orange-coloured flowers. It is of robust growth, and in favoured situations reaches the height of 6 feet. When it is in full flower the slopes of the Southern Alleghany Mountains are rendered highly attractive by reason of the great flame-coloured masses of this splendid plant, and are one of the great sights of the American Continent during the month of June.

R. CALIFORNICUM.—California. A good hardy species,

with broadly campanulate rosy-purple flowers, spotted with yellow.

R. CAMPANULATUM (*syn R. æruginosum*).—Sikkim, 1825. Small-growing species, rarely over 6 feet high, with elliptic leaves that are fawn-coloured on the undersides. The campanulate flowers are large and showy, rose or white and purple spotted, at the base of the three upper lobes. In this country it is fairly hardy, but suffers in very severe weather, unless planted in a sheltered site. There are several good varieties.

R. CAMPYLOCARPUM.—Sikkim, 1851. This has stood the winter uninjured in so many districts that it may at least be recommended for planting in favoured situations and by the seaside. The leaves are about 4 inches long, 2 inches wide, and distinctly undulated on the margins. Flowers bell-shaped, about 2 inches in diameter, and arranged in rather straggling terminal heads. They are sulphur-yellow, without markings, a tint distinct from any other known Indian species.

R. CATAWBIENSE.—Mountains from Virginia to Georgia, 1809. A bushy, free-growing species, with broadly oval leaves and large campanulate flowers, produced in compact, rounded clusters. They vary a good deal in colour, but lilac-purple is the typical shade. This is a very valuable species, and one that has given rise to a large number of beautiful varieties.

R. CHRYSANTHUM is a Siberian species (1796) of very dwarf, compact group, with linear-lanceolate leaves that are ferruginous on the underside, and beautiful golden-yellow flowers an inch in diameter. It is a desirable but scarce species.

R. COLLETTIANUM is an Afghanistan species, and one that may be reckoned upon as being perfectly hardy. It is of very dwarf habit, and bears an abundance of small white and faintly fragrant flowers. For planting on rockwork it is a valuable species.

R. DAHURICUM. — Dahuria, 1780. A small-growing, scraggy-looking species of about a yard high, with oval-oblong leaves that are rusty-tomentose on the undersides. The flowers, which are produced in February, are purple or violet, in twos or threes, and usually appear before the leaves. It is a sparsely-leaved species, and of greatest value on account of the flowers being produced so early in the season. One of the hardiest species in cultivation. R. dahuricum atro-virens is a beautiful and worthy variety because nearly evergreen.

R. DILITATUM.—Japan, 1855. This is of dwarf growth though spreading considerably, with reddish-tinted leaves and rose-coloured flowers. It is a beautiful, hardy species.

R. FERRUGINEUM.—Alpine Rose. Europe, 1752. This dwarf species, rarely exceeding a yard in height, occurs in abundance on the Swiss Alps, and generally where few other plants are to be found. It is a neat little compact shrub, with oblong-lanceolate leaves that are rusty-scaly on the undersides, and has terminal clusters of rosy-red flowers. There are several varieties, including myrtifolium, erectum, and hybridum.

R. FLAVUM (*syn Azalea pontica*).—Pontic Azalea. A native of Asia Minor (1793), is probably the commonest of the recognized species, and may frequently, in this country, be seen forming good round bushes of 6 feet in height, with hairy lanceolate leaves and large yellow flowers, though in this latter it varies considerably, orange and orange tinged with red being colours often present. It is of free growth in any good light peaty or sandy soil.

R. HIRSUTUM.—Alpine Rose. South Europe, 1656. Very near R. ferrugineum, but having ciliated leaves, with glands on both sides. R. hallense and R. hirsutiforme are intermediate forms of a natural cross between R. hirsutum and R. ferrugineum. They are handsome, small-growing, brightly-flowered plants, and worthy of culture.

R. INDICUM.—Indian Azalea. A native of China (1808),

and perfectly hardy in the more favoured portions of Southern England, where it looks healthy and happy out of doors, and blooms freely from year to year. This is the evergreen so-called Azalea that is so commonly cultivated in greenhouses, with long hirsute leaves and large showy flowers. R. indicum amœnum (*syn Azalea amœna*), as a greenhouse plant is common enough, but except in the South of England and Ireland it is not sufficiently hardy to withstand severe frost. The flowers are, moreover, not very showy, at least when compared with some of the newer forms, being dull magenta, and rather lax of habit.

R. KEWENSE (1874) is a beautiful hybrid that is valuable for its perfect hardihood and as succeeding in suburban districts. The flowers are pale-flesh colour and freely produced.

R. LEDIFOLIUM (*syns Azalea ledifolia* and *A. liliiflora*).—Ledum-leaved Azalea. China, 1819. A perfectly hardy shrub. The flowers are large and white, but somewhat flaunting. It is, however, a desirable species for massing in quantity, beside clumps of the pink and yellow-flowered kinds. Though introduced nearly three-quarters of a century ago, this is by no means a common plant in our gardens.

R. MACROSEPALUM.—Japan, 1870. A dwarf, hardy species, with pink, purple-spotted flowers.

R. MAXIMUM.—American Great Laurel. North America, 1756. This is a very hardy American species, growing in favoured localities from 10 feet to 15 feet high. Leaves oblong-lanceolate, slightly ferruginous beneath. Flowers rose and white, in dense clusters. There are several handsome varieties that vary to a wide extent in the size and colour of flowers. R. maximum album bears white flowers.

R. MOLLE (*syn Azalea mollis*), from Japan (1867), is a dwarf, deciduous species of neat growth, with flame-coloured flowers. It is very hardy, and a desirable acquisition to any collection of small-growing shrubs.

R. OCCIDENTALE (*syn Azalea occidentalis*), Western Azalea, is valuable in that the flowers are produced later than those of almost any other species. These are white, blotched with yellow at the base of the upper petals; and being produced when the leaves are almost fully developed, have a very pleasing effect, particularly as they are borne in great quantity, and show well above the foliage. This is a Californian species that has been found further west of the Rocky Mountains than any other member of the family.

R. PARVIFOLIUM (1877).—This is a pleasing and interesting species, with small, deep-green ovate leaves, and clusters of white flowers, margined with rose. It is of dwarf and neat growth, and well suited for planting on the rock garden.

R. PONTICUM.—Pontic Rhododendron, or Rose Bay. Asia Minor, 1763. This is the commonest species in cultivation, and although originally a native of the district by the Black or Pontic Sea, is now naturalized in many parts of Europe. It is the hardiest and least exacting of the large-flowered species, and is generally employed as a stock on which to graft the less hardy kinds. Flowers, in the typical species, pale purplish-violet and spotted. There is a great number of varieties, including white, pink, scarlet, and double-flowering.

R. PONTICUM AZALEOIDES (*syn. R. ponticum deciduum*), a hybrid between R. ponticum and a hardy Azalea, is a sub-evergreen form, with a compact habit of growth, and bearing loose heads of fragrant lavender-and-white flowers. It is quite hardy at Kew.

R. RACEMOSUM.—Central China, 1880. A neat little species, of dwarf, compact growth, from the Yunnan district of China. The flowers are pale pink edged with a deeper tint, about an inch across, and borne in dense terminal and axillary clusters. It has stood unharmed for several years in Southern England, so may be regarded as at least fairly hardy. Its neat dwarf growth, and flowering as it does when hardly a foot high, renders it a choice subject for the Alpine garden.

R. RHODORA (*syn Rhodora canadensis*).—North America, 1767. In general aspect this shrub resembles an Azalea, but it comes into flower long even before R. molle. Being deciduous, and producing its pretty purplish sweet-scented flowers in early spring, gives to the plant a particular value for gardening purposes, clumps of the shrub being most effective at the very time when flowers are at their scarcest. It thrives well in any peaty soil, and is quite hardy.

R. VASEYI.—Carolina, 1888. This is a hardy species of robust growth, which flowers freely even in a young state. The flowers are of a bright, clear pink with darker markings at the base of the upper lobes.

R. VISCOSUM (*syn Azalea viscosa*).—Clammy Azalea, or Swamp Honeysuckle. North America, 1734. This is one of the hardiest, most floriferous, and easily managed of the family. The white or rose and deliciously fragrant flowers are produced in great abundance, and impart when at their best quite a charm to the shrub. It delights in rather moist, peaty soil, and grows all the stronger and flowers all the more freely when surrounded by rising ground or tall trees at considerable distance away. The variety R. viscosum glaucum has leaves paler than those of the species ; and R. viscosum nitidum, of dwarf, compact growth, has leaves deep green on both sides.

R. WILSONI, a cross between R. ciliatum and R. glaucum, is of remarkably neat growth, and worthy of cultivation where small-sized kinds are a desideratum.

The following Himalayan species have been found to thrive well in the warmer parts of England, and in close proximity to the sea :—R. argenteum, R. arboreum, R.

Aucklandii, R. barbatum, R. ciliatum, R. campanulatum, R. cinnabarinum, R. Campbelli, R. campylocarpum, R. eximium, R. Fortunei, R. Falconeri, R. glaucum, R. Hodgsoni, R. lanatum, R. niveum, R. Roylei, R. Thompsoni, and R. Wallichii.

R. Ungernii and R. Smirnowii, from the Armenian frontier, are also worthy of culture, but they are at present rare in cultivation in this country; while our native R. procumbens (*syn Loiseleurea procumbens*), of dwarf growth and with bell-shaped pink flowers, is interesting.

R. YUNNANENSE (Yunnan, 1894) is of erect growth, perfectly hardy, and bearing white flowers, which are spotted with red at the base of the upper lobes.

Few hardy shrubs, it must be admitted, are more beautiful than these Rhododendrons, none flowering more freely or lasting longer in bloom. Their requirements are by no means hard to meet, light, peaty soil, or even good sandy loam, with a small admixture of decayed vegetable matter, suiting them well. Lime in any form must, however, be kept away both from Azaleas and Rhododendrons. They like a quiet, still place, where a fair amount of moisture is present in the air and soil.

HARDY HYBRID RHODODENDRONS.

GHENT AZALEAS, as generally known, from having been raised in Belgium, are a race of hybrids that have been produced by crossing the Asiatic R. ponticum with the various American species noted above, but particularly R. calendulaceum, R. nudiflorum, and R. viscosum, and these latter with one another. These have produced hybrids of almost indescribable beauty, the flowers of which range in colour from crimson and pink, through orange and yellow, to almost white.

Within the last few years quite an interesting race of Rhododendrons has been brought out, with double or hose-in-hose flowers, and very appropriately termed the Narcissiflora group. They include fully a dozen highly ornamental kinds, with flowers of varying shades of colour.

The following list includes some of the best and most beautiful of these varieties :—

- Alba marginata.
- Ardens.
- Astreans.
- Aurore-de-Royghen.
- Baron G. Pyke.
- Beauté Celeste.
- Belle Holdaway.
- Belle Merveille.
- Bijou des Amateurs.
- Cardinal.
- Charles Bowman.
- Comte de Flanders.
- Decus hortorum.
- Duc de Provence.
- Emperor Napoleon III.
- Eugenie.
- Fitz Quihou.
- Glorie de Belgique.
- Gloria Mundi.
- Gueldres Rose.
- Honneur de Flandre.
- Imperator.
- Jules Cæsar.
- La Superbe.
- Louis Hellebuyck.
- Madame Baumann.
- Marie Verschaffelt.
- Mathilde.
- Meteor.
- Nancy Waterer.
- Ne Plus Ultra.
- Optima.
- Pallas.
- Queen Victoria.
- Reine de Belges.
- Remarquable.
- Roi des Belges.
- Roi des Feux.
- Sinensis rosea.
- Sulphurea.
- Triumphans.
- Unique.
- Viscocephala.

Double-flowered Rhododendrons :—

- Bijou de Gendbrugge.
- Graf Von Meran.
- Heroine.
- Narcissiflora.
- Louis Aimée Van Houtte.
- Mina Van Houtte.
- Ophirié.
- Van Houttei.

Hardy Rhododendrons, garden varieties :—

Agamemnon.
Annie Dixwell.
Blanche Superbe.
Brilliant.
Cunninghamii.
Doncaster.
Kate Waterer.
Limbatum.
M. T. Masters.
Mrs. John Waterer.
Nobleanum coccineum.
Obtusa.
Pink Pearl.
Lady Clementine Mitford.
Princess William of Wurtemburg.
Prometheus.
Pulcherrimum.
Torlinianum.
Vesuvius.

Rhodora. See Rhododendron.

Rhodothamnus (Ericaceæ).

RHODOTHAMNUS CHAMÆCISTUS (*syn Rhododendron Chamæcistus*).—Ground Cistus. Alps of Austria and Bavaria, 1786. A very handsome shrub, of small growth, and widely distributed in Bavaria, Switzerland, and elsewhere. Planted in peaty soil and in a rather damp, shady situation it thrives best, the oval-serrate leaves, covered with white, villous hairs and pretty rosy flowers, giving it an almost unique appearance. It is a charming rock shrub and perfectly hardy.

Rhodotypos (Rosaceæ).

RHODOTYPOS KERRIOIDES.—White Kerria. Japan, 1866. A handsome, deciduous shrub, and one that is readily propagated, and comparatively cheap. It is distinct and pretty when in flower, and one of the hardiest and most accommodating of shrubs. The leaves are handsome, being deeply serrated and silky on the undersides, while the pure-white flowers are often about 2 inches across. It grows about 4 feet in height, and is a very distinct and desirable shrub.

Rhus (*Anacardiaceæ*).

Rhus cotinoides.—Alabama. This is a beautiful species which much resembles R. Cotinus in general appearance, but the oval leaves are about 4 inches long and assume a beautiful colour in autumn. The flowers are small and arranged in nearly sessile panicles.

R. Cotinus.—Smoke Plant, Wig Tree, or Venetian Sumach. Spain to Caucasus, 1656. On account of its singular appearance this shrub always attracts the attention of even the most unobservant in such matters. It is a spreading shrub, about 6 feet high, with rotundate, glaucous leaves on long petioles. The flowers are small and inconspicuous, but the feathery nature of the flower clusters, occasioned by the transformation of the pedicels and hairs into fluffy awns, renders this Sumach one of the most curious and attractive of hardy shrubs. Spreading about freely, this South European shrub should be allowed plenty of room so that it may become perfectly developed.

R. Glabra (*syns R. caroliniana, R. coccinea, R. elegans,* and *R. sanguinea*).—Smooth or Scarlet Sumach. North America, 1726. A smaller tree than the last, with leaves that are deep glossy-green above and whitish beneath. The male tree bears greenish-yellow flowers, and the female those of a reddish-scarlet, but otherwise no difference between the trees can be detected. R. glabra laciniata (Fern Sumach) is a distinct and handsome variety, with finely-cut, elegant leaves and a dwarf and compact habit of growth. The leaves are very beautiful, and resemble those of the Grevillea robusta. It is a worthy variety.

R. Michauxii.—United States, 1895. A beautiful, hardy, spreading shrub, with pyramidal panicles of bright-scarlet flowers which are clothed with a silky pubescens.

R. succedanea.—Red Lac Sumach. Japan, 1768. This is not often seen planted out, though in not a few places it succeeds perfectly well. It has elegant foliage, each leaf being 15 inches long, and divided into several pairs of leaflets. The flowers are greenish-yellow.

R. TOXICODENDRON.—Poison Oak or Poison Ivy. North America, 1640. This species is of half-scandent habit, with large, trifoliate leaves, which turn of various tints of red and crimson in the autumn, and loose panicles of greenish-yellow flowers. It is quite hardy, and seen to best advantage when allowed to run over large rockwork and tree stumps in partial shade. The variety R. toxicodendron radicans has ample foliage, and is suited for similar places to the last. The leaves turn bright yellow in the autumn.

R. TRICHOCARPA.—Japan, 1897. This is a tree of slender growth, and is of no particular value in an ornamental way. The leaves are unequally pinnate, and the flowers inconspicuous.

R. TYPHINA.—Stag's Horn Sumach, or Vinegar Tree. A native of North America (1629), and a very common shrub in our gardens, probably on account of its spreading rapidly by suckers. It is, when well grown, a handsome and distinct shrub or small tree, with large, pinnate, hairy leaves and shoots that are rendered very peculiar by reason of the dense hairs with which they are covered for some distance back. The dense clusters of greenish-yellow flowers are sure to attract attention, although they are by no means pretty. R. typhina viridiflora is the male-flowered form of this species, with green flowers.

R. VENENATA (*syn R. vernix*).—Poison Elder, Sumach, or Dogwood. North America, 1713. This is remarkable for its handsome foliage, and is the most poisonous species of the genus. The flowers are green in loose panicles.

All the Sumachs grow and flower freely in any good garden soil, indeed, in that respect they are not at all particular. They throw up shoots freely, so that increasing the stock is by no means difficult.

Rhynchospermum. See Trachelospermum.

Ribes (Saxifrageæ).

RIBES ALPINUM PUMILUM AUREUM.—Golden Mountain Currant. The ordinary green form is a native of Britain, of which the plant named above is a dwarf, golden-leaved variety. The flowers are yellow.

R. AUREUM.—Buffalo Currant. North-West America, 1812. In this species the leaves are lobed and irregularly toothed, while the flowers are yellow, or slightly reddish tinted. It is of rather slender and straggling growth. R. aureum præcox is an early-flowering variety; and R. aureum serotinum is valued on account of the flowers being produced much later than are those of the parent plant.

R. CEREUM (*syn R. inebrians*).—North America, 1827. One of the dwarfer-growing species of Flowering Currant, forming a low, dense bush of Gooseberry-like appearance, but destitute of spines. By May it is in full flower, and the blooms, borne in large clusters, have a pretty pinkish tinge. The foliage is small, neat, and of a tender green that helps to set off the pretty flowers to perfection. It is a native of North-West America, and perfectly hardy in every part of the country. Though not equal in point of floral beauty with our common flowering Currant, still the miniature habit, pretty and freely-produced pink-tinted flowers, and fresh green foliage will all help to make it an acquisition wherever planted. Like the other species of Ribes, the present plant grows and flowers very freely in any soil, and almost however poor.

R. FLORIDUM (*syns R. missouriense, R. Amincanum,* and *R. pennsylvanicum*).—American Wild Black Currant. North America, 1729. This should be included in all collections for its pretty autumnal foliage, which is of a bright purplish bronze.

R. GORDONIANUM (*syns R. Beatonii* and *R. Loudonii*) is a hybrid between R. aureum and R. sanguineum, and has reddish, yellow-tinged flowers, and partakes generally of the characters of both species.

R. MULTIFLORUM, Eastern Europe (1822), is another desirable species, with long, drooping racemes of greenish-yellow flowers, and small red berries.

R. PROSTRATUM (North America, 1812) is a good plant for the rockwork, with deeply cordate, lobed leaves and pretty erect racemes of yellowish flowers.

R. SANGUINEUM. — Flowering Currant. North-West America, 1826. An old inhabitant of our gardens, and well deserving of all that can be said in its favour as a beautiful spring-flowering shrub. It is of North American origin, with deep-red and abundantly-produced flowers. There are several distinct varieties as follows: R. sanguineum flore-pleno (Burning Bush), with perfectly double flowers, which are produced later and last longer than those of the species; R. sanguineum album, with pale-pink or almost white flowers; R. sanguineum atrorubens, with deeply-coloured flowers; R. sanguineum glutinosum and R. sanguineum grandiflorum, bearing compact clusters of flowers that are rosy-flesh coloured on the outside and white or pinky-white within.

R. SPECIOSUM.—Fuchsia-flowered Gooseberry. California, 1829. A Californian species, remarkable for being more or less spiny, and with flowers resembling some of the Fuchsias. They are crimson, and with long, protruding stamens. As a wall plant, where it often rises to 6 feet in height, this pretty and taking species is most often seen.

The flowering Currants are of unusually free growth, and are not at all particular about soil, often thriving well in that of a very poor description. They are increased readily from cuttings and by layers.

Robinia (Leguminosæ). See Halimodendron.

ROBINIA DUBIA (*syns R. echinata* and *R. ambigua*).—A very pretty garden hybrid form, said to have for its parentage R. Pseud-Acacia and R. viscosa. It is of quite tree-like growth and habit, with unusually short spines, and pea-green foliage. The flowers are produced pretty freely, and are of a pale-rose colour, and well set off by the light-green leaves, over which they hang in neat and compact spikes.

R. HISPIDA (*syn R. rosea*).—Rose Acacia. North America, 1743. Amongst large-growing shrubs this is certainly one of the most distinct and handsome, and at the same time one of the hardiest and readiest of culture. Under favourable conditions it grows about 16 feet high, with large oval or oblong leaflets, and having the young branches densely clothed with bristles. The flowers, which are individually larger than those of the False Acacia, are of a beautiful rosy-pink, and produced in June and July. It is a very ornamental, small-growing species, and one that is peculiarly suitable for planting where space is limited. R. hispida macrophylla (Large-leaved Rose Acacia) is rendered distinct by its generally more robust growth, and by its larger foliage and flowers. The species, however, varies a good deal in respect of the size of leaves and flowers.

R. NEO-MEXICANA.—New Mexico, 1891. This is a desirable species, with glaucous foliage and dense, clustered racemes of pale rose-coloured flowers.

R. PSEUD-ACACIA.—Common Locust, Bastard Acacia, or False Acacia. North America, 1640. A noble-growing and handsome tree, with smooth shoots, and stipules that become transformed into sharp, stiff spines. The flowers are in long racemes, pure white or slightly tinged with pink, and with a faint pleasing odour. This species has been sub-divided into a great number of varieties, some of which are very distinct, but the majority are not sufficiently so to warrant special attention. The following include the best and most popular kinds: R. Pseud-Acacia Decaisneana, a distinct form bearing light pinky flowers; R. Pseud-Acacia Bessoniana, with thornless branches and a dense head of refreshing pea-green foliage; R. Pseud-Acacia angustifolia, with narrow leaves; R. Pseud-Acacia aurea, a conspicuous but not very constant golden-leaved form; R. Pseud-Acacia inermis, of which there are weeping, upright, and broad-leaved forms, has narrow leaves that are glaucous beneath, and the characteristic spines of the species are wanting or rarely well developed. It is a small-growing, round-headed bush, and is usually seen as a standard grafted on the common type. R. Pseud-Acacia monophylla is very distinct, the leaves being entire instead of pinnate; while R. Pseud-Acacia crispa has curiously-curled foliage. Then there is the peculiar R. Pseud-Acacia tortuosa, of ungainly habit; R. Pseud-Acacia umbraculifera, with a spreading head; R. Pseud-Acacia sophoræfolia, the leaves of which resemble those of Sophora japonica; and R. Pseud-Acacia amorphæfolia, with very large foliage when compared with the parent tree. The above may be taken as the most distinct and desirable forms of the False Acacia, but there are many others, such as R. Pseud-Acacia colutoides, R. Pseud-Acacia semperflorens, and R. Pseud-Acacia Rhederi, all more or less distinct from the typical tree.

R. VISCOSA (*syn R. glutinosa*).—Clammy Locust. North America, 1797. This is a small-growing tree, and readily distinguished by the clammy bark of the younger shoots. Flowers in short racemes, and of a beautiful rose-pink, but varying a good deal in depth of tint. It is a valuable species for ornamental planting, and flowers well even in a young state.

Few soils would seem to come amiss to the Acacias,

but observations made in many parts of the country conclusively prove that the finest specimens are growing on light, rich loam overlaying a bed of gravel. They are propagated from seed, by layers, or by grafting.

Romneya (Papaveraceæ).

Romneya Coulteri.—Californian Tree Poppy. California, 1875. This is sometimes referred to as an herbaceous subject, but as it rarely dies down to the ground, hardly comes within the definition of such, and has of late years been included as a shrubby plant. It is a charming shrub, with large, deeply-cut glaucous foliage, and flowers of a peculiarly delicate texture, pure white with conspicuous yellow stamens. Many of the individual flowers measure 8 inches in diameter, and when, as is often the case on established specimens, a dozen flowers are open at the same time, the plant has a charming and beautiful effect. A southern aspect, at the foot of a wall, affords an ideal site for this Romneya, but it must have an abundant supply of water, while an occasional application of weak liquid manure causes it to send up vigorous shoots from the base, and these shoots produce the finest flowers. It is not at all particular as to soil, and has succeeded well in good loam to which a little peat was added.

Rosa (Rosaceæ).

Rosa alba.—This is a supposed garden hybrid between R. canina and R. gallica (1597). It has very glaucous foliage, and large flowers, which vary according to the variety from pure white to rose.

R. alpina (Europe, 1683) grows about a yard high, with doubly serrated leaves, the young stems prickly, and solitary pink or rosy flowers. There are several varieties, including pendulina and pyrenaica.

R. BANKSIÆ (China, 1809) is a desirable species, with numerous small, nodding, double-white, scented flowers. It will climb to 20 feet in height.

R. BRACTEATA (Macartney Rose), R. PALUSTRIS (Marsh Rose), and R. MICROPHYLLA (small-leaved Rose), belong to that section supplied with floral leaves or bracts, and shaggy fruit. They are of compact growth, with neat, shining leaves, the flowers of the first-mentioned being rose or carmine, and those of the other two pure white.

R. CANINA.—Dog Rose. Our native Roses have now been reduced to five species, of which the present is one of the number. It is a straggling shrub, 6 feet or 8 feet high, and armed with curved spines. Flowers sweet-scented, pink or white, and solitary, or in twos or threes at the branch tips. There are many varieties.

R. CENTIFOLIA. — Hundred-leaved, or Cabbage Rose. Orient, 1596. A beautiful, sweetly-scented species, growing to 6 feet in height, and having leaves that are composed of from three to five broadly ovate, toothed leaflets. The flowers are solitary, or two or three together, drooping, and of a rosy hue, but differing in tint to a considerable extent. This species has varied very much, principally through the influences of culture and crossing, the three principal and marked variations being size, colour, and clothing of the calyx tube. There are the common Provence Roses, the miniature Provence or Pompon Roses, and the Moss Rose—all of which are merely races of R. centifolia.

R. DAMASCENA.—Damask Rose. Orient, 1573. A bushy shrub varying from 2 feet to 8 feet in height according to cultural treatment and age. The flowers are white or red, large, borne in corymbose clusters, and produced in great profusion during June and July. The varieties that have arisen under cultivation by seminal variations, hybridization, or otherwise, are exceedingly numerous. Those now grown are mostly double, and a large proportion of them are light in colour. They include the quatre saisons and the true York and Lancaster. The flowers are highly fragrant, and, like those of R. centifolia and other species, are used indiscriminately for the purpose of making rose-water. The species is distinguished from R. centifolia by its larger prickles, elongated fruit, and long, reflexed sepals.

R. FEROX.—North Asia. This species bears flowers in clusters of two and three together, terminating the branches. The petals are white with a yellow base. The branches are erect, and thickly crowded with prickles of unequal size.

R. GALLICA.—The French, or Gallic Rose. Europe and Western Asia. This Rose forms a bushy shrub 2 feet to 3 feet high, and has been so long grown in British gardens that the date of its introduction has been lost in obscurity. It is doubtless the red Rose of ancient writers, but at present the flowers may be red, crimson, or white, and there are varieties of all intermediate shades. Several variegated or striped Roses belong here, including Gloria Mundi, a popular favourite often but erroneously grown under the name of York and Lancaster. They all flower in June and July, and, together with other kinds that flower about the same time, are generally known as summer or old-fashioned garden Roses.

R. HEMISPHÆRICA (*syn R. sulphurea*).—Orient, 1629. A bushy plant growing from 4 feet to 6 feet high, and bearing large double yellow flowers.

R. INDICA.—Common China, or Monthly Rose. Introduced from China, near Canton, in 1789, but the native country is not known with certainty. The flowers of the plant when first introduced were red and generally semi-double, but the varieties now vary through all shades of blush, rose, and crimson, and the plant varies exceedingly in height, in its different forms 1 foot to 20 feet in height. The Monthly Roses form bushes generally about 2 feet high or a little over. The Noisette and Tea Roses, with several other more or less distinct types, belong here, but as most of them are well known and otherwise well cared for, it is unnecessary to dwell upon them in detail beyond the two varieties here given, which should not be overlooked.

R. INDICA MINIMA (*syns R. semperflorens minima, R. Lawrenceana,* and *R. minima*).—Fairy, or Miniature Rose. China, 1810. A beautiful little Rose that rarely exceeds a height of 4 inches or 5 inches. The flowers are about the size of a half-crown, and somewhat after the York and Lancaster as regards colouring, though not, perhaps, so distinctly marked, and are produced in abundance. For the rock garden it is one of the most desirable, and being perfectly hardy and readily raised from seed still further adds to its value.

R. INDICA SEMPERFLORENS (*syns R. bengalensis* and *R. diversifolia*).—The Ever-flowering China Rose. China, 1789. A somewhat spreading bush, with slender branches, armed with curved prickles. Leaves composed of three or five leaflets and tinted with purple. Flowers almost scentless, solitary, semi-double, and of a bright and showy crimson.

R. LUCIÆ (*syn R. Wichuriana*).—Japan and China, 1880. A beautiful prostrate shrub, with ovate leaves and a rich profusion of solitary, scented white flowers.

R. LUTEA (*syn R. Eglanteria*).—The Austrian Brier, or Yellow Eglantine. South Europe, 1596. This belongs to the Sweet Brier section, and is a bush of from 3 feet to 6 feet high, with shining dark-green leaves, and large, cup-shaped flowers that are yellow or sometimes tinged with reddish-brown within. The Scarlet Austrian Brier (R. lutea punicea) is a handsome variety, with the upper surface of the petals scarlet and the under surface yellow. The Penzance Briers, of which there are now nearly a score of varieties, are well worthy of culture, and grow vigorously in any good garden soil.

R. POMIFERA.—This European species is remarkable for the large red or purplish fruit which it usually bears in abundance, and for which the plant is most in favour. The pinky, usually solitary flowers are of no particular interest.

R. REPENS (*syn R. arvensis*).—Field Rose. Europe (Britain). This species bears white flowers that are produced in threes or fours, rarely solitary. The whole plant is usually of weak and straggling growth, with shining leaves.

R. RUBIGINOSA (*syn R. Eglanteria*). — Eglantine, or Sweet Brier. This species has pink flowers and clammy leaves, which are glandular on the under surface, and give out a fragrant smell by which it may be recognized.

R. RUGOSA (*syn R. ferox of Bot. Reg.*), a Japanese species, and its variety R. rugosa alba, are beautiful shrubs that have proved themselves perfectly hardy and well suit for extensive culture in this country. They are of stiff, shrubby habit, about 4 feet high, and with branches thickly clothed with spines becoming brown with age. Leaflets oval in shape, deep green, with the upper surface rough to the touch, the undersides densely tomentose. Flowers single, fully 3 inches in diameter, the petals of good substance, and white or rose-coloured. The fruit is large, larger than that of perhaps any other rose, and of a bright red when fully ripe. In so far as beauty of fruit is concerned, this Rose has certainly no rival, and whether for the rockwork or open border it must be classed amongst the most useful and beautiful of hardy shrubs. R. rugosa is a capital hedge plant, and being a true species it is readily propagated from seed. R. rugosa Kamtschatika is a deep-red flowered form with deciduous spines.

R. SEMPERVIRENS.—Evergreen Rose. South Europe and India, 1529. A climbing species, with long, slender branches, armed with hooked prickles. Leaves evergreen, shining, and composed of from five to seven leaflets. The clustered flowers are white and sweet-scented.

R. SPINOSISSIMA (*syn R. pimpinellifolia*). — Burnet, or Scotch Rose. A small bush about 2 feet high, of neat growth, with small leaves, and pink or white flowers that are solitary at the branch ends.

R. VILLOSA.—Downy Rose. Europe (Britain). This species is of erect bushy growth, with the leaflets softly downy on both sides. Flowers white or pale pink, succeeded by globular fruits, that are more or less covered with fine hair or prickles. Strong, stiffish loam will suit their wants in the way of soil.

Rosmarinus (Labiatæ).

ROSMARINUS OFFICINALIS.—Common Rosemary. Mediterranean region, 1848. A familiar garden shrub, of dense growth, with dusky grey-green linear leaves and pale-blue or white flowers. There is a golden and a silver leaved variety, named respectively R. officinalis foliis-aureis and R. officinalis foliis-argenteis; as also one distinguished by having broader foliage than the species, and named R. officinalis latifolius.

Rubus (Rosaceæ).

RUBUS ARCTICUS.—Arctic Regions of both hemispheres. An interesting species about 6 inches high, with trifoliate leaves and deep-red flowers. For Alpine gardening it is a valuable species of dwarf growth.

R. AUSTRALIS, from New Zealand, is a very prickly species, with the leaves reduced to their stalks and the midribs of three leaflets, while the panicled flowers are pink or whitish and fragrant. Not being very hardy it is usually seen as a wall plant.

R. BIFLORUS.—Himalayas, 1818. A tall-growing species with whitish, spiny stems, and simple three-lobed leaves that are tomentose on the undersides. The flowers are thickly produced, pure white, and render the plant highly attractive and of great beauty.

R. DELICIOSUS.—This Rocky Mountain Bramble (1870) is a very worthy species, with three or five-lobed (not pinnate) leaves, and large pure-white flowers that are each about 2 inches in diameter, and produced in profusion from the leaf-axils. For ornamental planting this may be placed in the first rank of the family to which it belongs.

R. FRUTICOSUS.—Common Bramble, or Blackberry. Of this well-known native species there are several worthy varieties, of which the double-flowered are especially worth notice, blooming as they do in the latter part of summer. R. fruticosus flore albo-pleno (Double white-flowered Bramble) and R. fruticosus flore roseo-pleno (Double red-flowered Bramble) are very pretty and showy varieties, and well worth including in any collection. There is a pretty variegated-leaved form of the common Bramble, known as R. fruticosus variegatus.

R. LACINIATUS, Cut-leaved Bramble, might also be included on account of its profusion of white flowers and neatly divided foliage.

R. LEUCODERMIS, from Oregon, is an interesting species, with white flowers, and stems that appear as if white-washed.

R. NUTKANUS.—North America, 1826. This has large white flowers, but otherwise it resembles R. odoratus.

R. ODORATUS. — Purple flowering Raspberry. North America, 1700. The sweet-scented Virginian Raspberry forms a rather dense, upright-growing bush, fully 4 feet high, with large broadly five-lobed and toothed leaves, that are more or less viscid, sweet-scented, and deciduous. The leaves are placed on long, hairy, viscid footstalks.

Flowers in terminal corymbs, large and nearly circular, purplish-red in colour, and composed of five broad, round petals. The fruit, which is rarely produced in this country, is velvety and amber-coloured. It is a very ornamental species, the ample Maple-like leaves and large flowers rendering it particularly attractive in summer. The leaves, and not the flowers as is generally supposed, are sweetly scented.

R. PHŒNICOLASIUS (the Japanese Wine-berry) has showy white flowers, large scarlet fruit, and foliage covered with conspicuous red hairs.

R. ROSÆFOLIUS.—Rose-leaved Raspberry. Himalayas, 1811. Another half-hardy species, and only suited for planting against sunny walls. Leaves pinnate, finer than those of the Raspberry. R. r. coronarius, with semi-double white flowers, is better than the type.

R. SPECTABILIS.—The Salmon Berry. North America, 1827. Grows about 6 feet high, with ternate or tri-lobate leaves that are very thickly produced. Flowers usually bright red or purplish-coloured, and placed on long pendulous footstalks. It is of very dense growth, occasioned by the number of suckers sent up from the roots.

There are also some of the so-called American Brambles well worthy of attention, two of the best being Kittatiny and Lawton's. The Loganberry, a hybrid between a red Raspberry and an American variety, is both hardy and prolific, but is yet scarce. The fruit is like an enormous Raspberry.

The brambles are particularly valuable shrubs, as owing to their dense growth they may be used for a variety of purposes, but especially for covering unsightly objects or banks. They are all wonderfully floriferous, and succeed admirably even in very poor and stony soils. Increase is readily obtained either from root suckers or by layering.

Ruscus (Liliaceæ). See Danæ.

RUSCUS ACULEATUS.—Butcher's Broom, Pettigree and Pettigrue. Europe (Britain) and North Africa. This is a native evergreen shrub, with rigid cladodes which take the place of leaves, and not very showy greenish flowers appearing about May. For the bright-red berries, which are as large as small marbles, it is alone worth cultivating, while it is one of the few shrubs that grow at all satisfactorily beneath the shade of our larger trees.

R. HYPOPHYLLUM. — Double Tongue. Mediterranean region, 1640. This species has the flowers on the undersides of the leaf-like branches; and its variety R. H. Hypoglossum has them on the upper side. Both are of value for planting in the shade.

R. RACEMOSUS. See DANÆ.

Sambucus (Caprifoliaceæ).

SAMBUCUS CALIFORNICA.—Californian Elder. A rare species as yet, but one that from its elegant growth and duration of flowers is sure, when better known, to become widely distributed.

S. CANADENSIS.—Canada, 1761. This grows about 5 feet high, with pinnate leaves, and white, nearly scentless, flowers, which are succeeded by deep bluish-black berries.

S. GLAUCA has its herbaceous parts covered with a thick pubescence; leaves pubescent on both sides, and with yellow flowers produced in umbels.

S. NIGRA.—Common Elder. Bourtry, or Bour tree. Although one of our commonest native trees, the Elder must rank amongst the most ornamental if only for its large compound cymes of white or yellowish-white flowers, and ample bunches of shining black berries. There are, however, several varieties that should be largely cultivated, such as S. nigra foliis aureis (Golden Elder), S. nigra fructu albo (White Fruited), S. nigra laciniata (Cut-leaved Elder), S. nigra argentea (Silver-leaved Elder), S. nigra rotundifolia (Round-leaved Elder), the names of which will be sufficient for the purposes of recognition.

S. RACEMOSA.—Scarlet-berried Elder. South Europe and Siberia, 1596. This is almost a counterpart of our native species, but instead of black the berries are brilliant scarlet. It is a highly ornamental shrub, bearing white flowers in April and May, but it is rather exacting, requiring for its perfect growth a cool and moist situation. Of this there is a cut-leaved form, named S. racemosa serratifolia.

S. ROSÆFLORA is said to be a seedling from S. glauca, but differs in many important points from the parent. It has smooth shoots and branches, ovate-acuminate leaves that are downy beneath, and flowers rose-coloured without and white within. They are produced in short, spike-like clusters, and are almost destitute of smell. The reddish rings at the insertion of the leaves is another distinguishing feature.

For freedom of growth in almost every class of soil, and readiness with which they may be increased, the more showy kinds of Elder are well worthy of attention.

Santolina (Compositæ).

SANTOLINA CHAMÆCYPARISSUS. — South Europe, 1573 (Cotton Lavender). A small-growing and densely-branched shrub, with a hoary pubescence. The leaves are thickly arranged, alternate, and with several rows of short obtuse teeth pointing in all directions. The rounded heads of yellow flowers render this shrub distinct about midsummer, while the whole greyish appearance causes it to look out of the common. In light, rich soil it is quite at home.

There are three varieties, S. C. incana, S. C. squarrosa, and S. C. tomentosa.

Schizandra (Magnoliaceæ).

Schizandra chinensis.—Northern China, 1860. This is a climbing shrub, with oval, bright-green leaves and showy carmine flowers. For clothing arbors and walls it may prove of use, but it is as yet rare in cultivation.

S. coccinea, from North America (1806), is another uncommon species in which the leaves are oblong and petiolate, and the flowers red or scarlet. For purposes similar to the last this species may be employed.

Schizophragma (Saxifrageæ).

Schizophragma hydrangeoides.—Climbing Hydrangea. Japan, 1879. As yet this is an uncommon shrub, and allied to the Hydrangea. It is of slender growth, the stems rooting into the support, and with pinky-white flowers. As an ornamental climber it is of no great value, and requires a favoured spot to grow it at all satisfactorily.

S. integrifolia is a desirable shrub of recent introduction, with ovate-lanceolate leaves often 8 inches long, and the inflorescence surrounded with conspicuous white bracts.

Shepherdia (Elœagnaceæ).

Shepherdia argentea.—Beef Suet Tree, or Rabbit Berry. North America, 1820. This shrub is rendered of particular interest on account of the intense silvery hue of the foliage. The leaves are narrow and lanceolate, silvery on both sides, and dotted over with rusty-brown scales beneath. The flowers, which are produced in April, are small and yellow, unisexual, or each sex on a distinct plant. Berries scarlet, about the size of red Currants, and ripe about September.

S. canadensis.—North America, 1759. This is a small-growing, straggling species, fully 4 feet high, and clothed with rusty scales. The leaves are ovate or elliptic, and green above, and the flowers of an inconspicuous yellow, succeeded by orange-red berries. They thrive well by the seaside, in light, rich soil.

Sida. See Plagianthus.

Skimmia (Rutaceæ).

Skimmia Fortunei.—Japan, 1845. This is a neat-growing shrub, with glossy, laurel-like leaves, white or greenish-white flowers, and an abundance of scarlet berries in autumn. It succeeds best in a somewhat shady situation, and when planted in not too heavy peaty soil, but where abundance of not stagnant moisture is present.

S. japonica (of Thunberg) (*syn S. oblata*).—Japan, 1864. A neat-growing, evergreen shrub, with rather larger and more showy leaves than the former, and spikes of pretty whitish, sweetly-scented flowers. The female form of this is usually known as S. fragrans. What is usually known as S. oblata ovata, and S. oblata Veitchii, are only forms of the true S. japonica; while S. fragrantissima is the male of the same species. The beautiful, berried plant that has been exhibited under the name of S. Foremanii, and which is of very vigorous growth, and produces pyramidal spikes of sweetly-scented flowers, is probably S. japonica, or a seminal variety. Another variety sent out under the name of S. macrophylla has unusually large leaves; and another named S. Rogersi produces fruit very abundantly.

S. Laureola (*syn Limonia Laureola*), from the Himalayas, is an uncommon species, with very fragrant pale-yellow flowers, and oblong-lanceolate leaves often 5 inches long.

S. rubella (China, 1874) is another member of the family that has greenish-white, sweet-scented flowers and pinky buds, and which, when better known, will be largely planted.

All the Skimmias succeed in good yellow loam to which a dash of peat has been added, and in a cool, shadyish situation.

Smilax (Smilaceæ).

Smilax aspera.—The Prickly Ivy. South Europe, 1648. A trailing-habited shrub, with prickly stems, ovate, spiny-toothed, evergreen leaves, and rather unattractive flowers. There are other hardy species from North America, including S. Bona-nox (better known as S. tamnoides, 1739), S. rotundifolia, and S. herbacea, the first being the most desirable, and bearing greenish-white flowers. S. aspera mauritanica is a hardy and beautiful variety, with greenish-yellow fragrant flowers, but one that is rare in cultivation, with long, wiry shoots, and well adapted for wall or trellis covering. They all require favoured situations, else the growth is short, and the plants stunted and meagre in appearance, while for soil a good sandy loam is preferred.

Solanum (Solanaceæ).

Solanum crispum. — Potato-tree. A native of Chili, 1824, and not very hardy, except in the coast regions of England and Ireland. It grows stout and bushy, often in favoured places rising to the height of 12 feet, and has large clusters of purple-blue fragrant flowers that are succeeded by small white or yellowish-white berries. This is a decidedly ornamental shrub that should be cultivated wherever a suitable place can be spared. It bears hard pruning back with impunity, and succeeds in any light, rich, loamy soil.

S. DULCAMARA.—Bitter Sweet, and Woody Nightshade. This is a native plant, and one of great beauty when seen clambering over a fence or bank. It has long, flexuous stems, and large clusters of purple flowers, which are rendered all the more conspicuous by the showy yellow anthers. The scarlet fruit is very effective. It sometimes, as in Regent's Park, London, rises to a height of 16 feet, with woody stems fully an inch in diameter.

S. JASMINOIDES, with its pure-white flowers and yellow stamens, is valuable for wall purposes.

Sophora (Leguminosæ).

SOPHORA JAPONICA (*syn Styphnolobium japonicum*).—Chinese or Japanese Pagoda-tree. China and Japan, 1763. A large deciduous tree, with elegant pinnate foliage, and clusters of small greenish-white flowers produced in September. Leaves dark-green, and composed of about eleven leaflets. S. japonica pendula is one of the most constant of weeping trees, and valuable for planting in certain well-chosen spots on the lawn or in the park.

S. TETRAPTERA.—New Zealand, 1772. This requires protection in any but favoured situations. It is a valuable species, having numerous leaflets, and bearing racemes of very showy yellow flowers. S. tetraptera microphylla is a smaller-leaved variety, with ten to forty pairs of leaflets, and is known in gardens under the names of Edwardsia Macnabiana and E. tatraptera microphylla. Sandy loam and wall protection are necessities.

Sorbus. See Pyrus.

Spartium (Leguminosæ).

SPARTIUM JUNCEUM (*syn S. acutifolium*).—Spanish, or Rush Broom. Mediterranean region and Canary Isles, 1548. This resembles our common Broom, but the slender Rush-like branches are not angular, and usually destitute of leaves. The fragrant yellow flowers are produced abundantly in racemes, and when at their best impart to the shrub a very striking and beautiful appearance. For planting in poor, sandy or gravelly soils, or amongst stones and shingle, and where only a very limited number of shrubs could be got to grow, the Spanish Broom will be found an excellent and valuable plant. It is a native of Southern Europe, and is quite hardy all over the country. Propagated from seed.

Spiræa (Rosaceæ). See Neillia and Exochorda.

SPIRÆA ARBUSCULA.—Washington, 1897. This is an alpine shrub, with erect, wiry stems, and small, compact corymbs of the brightest rosy-red flowers.

S. BELLA.—Pretty-flowered Spiræa. Himalayas, 1820. The reddish stems of this rather tall-growing species are of interest, and render the plant distinct. Leaves ovate, acute, and serrated, and tormentose beneath. Flowers in spreading corymbs, of a very beautiful rose colour, and at their best from the middle of May till the middle of June. S. bella alba has white flowers.

S. BLUMEI.—Blume's Spiræa. Japan. This is a Japanese species, growing 4 feet or 5 feet high, with small, ovate, bluntly-pointed leaves, and white flowers arranged in compact terminal cymes. It is a good and worthy species for ornamental planting.

S. BULLATA (*syn S. crispifolia*).—Japan. This will ever be accounted valuable for the rock garden, owing to its very dwarf habit and extreme floriferousness. It bears tiny bunches of bright rose-coloured flowers, and these look all the more charming owing to the miniature size of the shrub, its average height being about 12 inches. A very interesting and valuable rock shrub, and one that no doubt about its perfect hardihood need be entertained.

S. CANA.—Hoary-leaved Spiræa. Croatia, 1825. This is a small, spreading shrub that rarely rises to more than 18 inches in height, with small, ovate, hoary leaves, and pretty white flowers arranged in corymbs. For rockwork planting it is one of the most valuable species, growing freely and producing its showy flowers in abundance. Quite hardy.

S. CANTONIENSIS (*syn S. Reevesiana*).—Reeve's Spiræa. Japan, 1843. An evergreen or sub-evergreen species, growing 3 feet high, with lanceolate leaves on long footstalks, and large, pure-white flowers arranged in terminal corymbs and placed on long peduncles.

S. CHAMÆDRIFOLIA (*syn S. ceanothifolia*).—Germander-leaved Spiræa. South-Eastern Europe to Japan, 1789. Grows about a yard high, with ovate, pubescent leaves, and white flowers. It varies widely in the shape and size of leaves. S. chamædrifolia ulmifolia (Elm-leaved Spiræa), a twiggy shrub, 3 feet high, with broad leaves and white flowers, is from Siberia. S. chamædrifolia cratægifolia (Hawthorn-leaved Spiræa) is of stout, half-erect growth, with rather stiff glaucous leaves that are oval in shape, and bright-red or pink flowers in fastigiate panicles. From Siberia (1790), and flowering at mid-summer.

S. DECUMBENS (*syn S. nana*).—Decumbent Spiræa. Tyrol. This is the smallest-growing of the shrubby Spiræas, rarely attaining to a greater height than 12 inches. It is a neat growing plant, with small oval leaves and white pedunculate flowers. For planting on the rockwork or in the front line of the shrubbery this is an invaluable shrub, and soon forms a neat and pretty specimen. It is perfectly hardy.

S. ~~DISCOLOR~~ ARIÆFOLIA (*syn S. ariæfolia*).—White Beam-leaved Spiræa. North-West America, 1827. This forms a dense, erect shrub about 6 feet high, with elliptic-oblong leaves, and clothed beneath with a whitish tomentum. The flowers are in large, terminal, slender-stalked panicles, and white or yellowish-white. It is one of the handsomest species in cultivation, the neat and yet not stiff habit, and pretty, plume-like tufts of nodding flowers making it a general favourite with the cultivators of hardy shrubs. Flowers about mid-summer. In rich soils, and where partially shaded from cold winds, it thrives best.

S. DOUGLASII.—Douglas's Spiræa. North-West America. This has long, obovate-lanceolate leaves, that are white with down on the under surface, and bears dense, oblong, terminal panicles of rosy flowers. S. Douglasii Nobleana (Noble's Spiræa) is a variety of great beauty, growing about a yard high, with large leaves often 4 inches long, and looser panicles of purple-red flowers. Flowering in July. The variety was introduced from California in 1859.

S. FISSA. Split-leaved Spiræa. Mexico, 1839. A stout, erect-growing shrub, about 8 feet high, with rather small leaves, angular, downy branches, and long, loose, terminal panicles of small and greenish-white flowers. The leaves are wedge-shaped at the base, and when young have the lateral incisions split into a pair of unequal and very sharp teeth. Flowering in May and June. In the South and West of England it thrives best.

S. HENRYI.—Of recent introduction, this is a promising species with ovate leaves and densely produced small white flowers. It is of Chinese origin, and is doing well in a sandy loam and warm position.

S. HYPERICIFOLIA (*syn S. flagellata*).—Asia Minor, 1640. A wiry twiggy shrub, fully 4 feet high, with entire leaves, and small white flowers produced in umbels at the tips of the last year's shoots. It is a pretty and desirable species.

S. JAPONICA (*syns S. callosa* and *S. Fortunei*).—Japanese Spiræa. China and Japan, 1859. This is a robust species about a yard high, with large lanceolate leaves, and small, rosy-red flowers arranged in corymbose heads. Flowering at mid-summer. There are several fine varieties of this species, including S. japonica alba, a compact bush about a foot high with white flowers; S. japonica rubra differs from the type in having dark-red flowers; S. japonica splendens is a free-flowering dwarf plant, with peach-coloured flowers, and suitable for forcing; and S. japonica superba has dark rose-red flowers. S. Bumalda is a closely allied form, if not a mere variety of S. japonica; it is of dwarf habit, with dark reddish-purple flowers.

S. LÆVIGATA (*syns S. altaicensis* and *S. altaica*).—Smooth Spiræa. Siberia, 1774. A stout, spreading shrub about a yard high, with large, oblong-lanceolate, smooth, and stalkless leaves. The white flowers are arranged in racemose panicles, and produced in May.

S. LINDLEYANA.—Lindley's Spiræa. Himalayas. A handsome, tall-growing species, growing from 6 feet to 8 feet high, with very large pinnate leaves and pretty white flowers in large terminal panicles. It is the largest-leaved Spiræa in cultivation, and forms a stately, handsome specimen, which produces its showy flowers in great quantities. Flowering at the end of summer.

S. MEDIA (*syns S. confusa* and *S. oblongifolia*).—Northern Asia, etc. The pure-white flowers of this species are very freely produced in corymbs along the shoots of the previous season during the months of June and July. The lanceolate, elliptic leaves are serrate, or the smaller ones toothed near the apex only. Within the past few years the species has been brought into prominence for forcing purposes, for which it is admirably suited. It forms an upright, branching bush usually about 3 feet high, and is best known under the name of S. confusa.

S. PRUNIFOLIA.—China and Japan, 1845. A twiggy-branched shrub, growing 4 feet or 5 feet high, with oval, Plum-like leaves and white flowers. There is a double-flowering variety named S. prunifolia flore-pleno, which is both distinct and beautiful.

S. ROTUNDIFOLIA.—Round-leaved Spiræa. Cashmere, 1839. A slender-branched shrub, having downy shoots and round, blunt leaves, flowering in July.

S. SALICIFOLIA.—Willow-leaved Spiræa. Europe, and naturalized in Britain. An erect-growing, densely-branched shrub, with smooth shoots, which usually spring directly from the ground. Leaves large, lanceolate, smooth, doubly serrated, and produced plentifully. Flowers red or rose-coloured, and arranged in short, thyrsoid panicles. It flowers in July and August. S. salicifolia carnea has flesh-coloured flowers ; S. salicifolia paniculata has white flowers ; and S. salicifolia grandiflora has pink flowers as large again as the type. S. salicifolia alpestris (Mountain Spiræa) grows fully 2 feet high, with lanceolate, finely-toothed leaves and loose, terminal panicles of pink or red flowers. From Siberia, and flowering in autumn. S. salicifolia latifolia (*syn S. carpinifolia*), the Hornbeam-leaved Spiræa, is a white-flowered variety, with leaves resembling those of the Hornbeam. From North America.

S. SORBIFOLIA.—Sorbus-leaved Spiræa. Siberia, 1759. A handsome, stout species, 4 feet high, with large, pinnate, bright-green leaves, and small, white, sweetly-scented flowers produced in thyrsoid panicles.

S. THUNBERGII.—Thunberg's Spiræa. Japan. The white flowers of this species smell somewhat like those of the Hawthorn, and are freely produced on the leafless, twiggy stems in March or early in April, according to the state of the weather. They are borne in axillary clusters from buds developed in the previous autumn, and are very welcome in spring, long before the others come into bloom. The bush varies from 1 foot to 3 feet high, and is clothed with linear-lanceolate, sharply serrated leaves.

S. TOMENTOSA.—Tomentose Spiræa. North America, 1736. This species grows 2 feet or 3 feet high, has rusty tomentose shoots and leaves, and large, dense, compound spikes of showy red flowers. Flowering in summer.

S. TRILOBATA (*syn S. triloba*).—Three-lobed Spiræa. Altaian Alps, 1801. This is a distinct species with horizontally arranged branches, small, roundish, three-lobed leaves, and white flowers arranged in umbel-like corymbs. It flowers in May, and is quite hardy.

S. UMBROSA (Shady Spiræa) and S. EXPANSA (Expanded-flowered Spiræa), the former from Northern India and the latter from Nepaul, are well suited for planting in somewhat shady situations, and are very ornamental species. The first-mentioned grows about a foot high, with rather large leaves, and cymes of white flowers on long, slender footstalks; while S. expansa has pink flowers, and lanceolate, coarsely serrated leaves.

There are other valuable-flowering kinds, such as S. capitata, with ovate leaves and white flowers; S. pikowiensis, a rare species with white flowers; S. cuneifolia, with wedge-shaped leaves and panicles of pretty white flowers; and S. vacciniæfolia, a dwarf-growing species, with small ovate, serrulated leaves and showy, pure-white flowers. S. betulifolia and S. chamædrifolia flexuosa are worthy forms of free growth and bearing white flowers. The Spiræas succeed in almost any garden soil, probably preferring a rich, sandy loam.

Stachyurus (Ternstromiaceæ).

STACHYURUS PRÆCOX.—China and Japan. A little-known but beautiful deciduous shrub of medium height, with ovate-lanceolate leaves 4 inches to 6 inches long, and long, drooping racemes of pale-yellow flowers produced in early March. Peaty loam and an open situation.

Staphylea (Sapindaceæ).

STAPHYLEA COLCHICA.—Colchican Bladder Nut. Caucasus. This is a very distinct shrub, about 6 feet high, with large clusters of showy white flowers. Being quite hardy, and very ornamental, this species is worthy the attention of planters.

S. COULOMBIERI (1887) is a garden variety intermediate between S. Colchica and S. pinnata, and differing from the former in its more globular flowers and later period of flowering.

S. PINNATA.—Job's Tears, or St. Anthony's Nut. South Europe. This is a straggling shrub, from 6 feet to 8 feet high, with white, racemose flowers, succeeded by bladder-like capsules.

S. TRIFOLIA.—North America, 1640. This is distinguished by its large white flowers and trifoliate leaves. It is the American Bladder Nut, but, like the latter, can hardly be included amongst ornamental plants.

All the Bladder Nuts grow freely in good light, dampish loam.

Stauntonia (Berberideæ).

STAUNTONIA HEXAPHYLLA.—China and Japan, 1876. This evergreen twining shrub is not to be generally recommended, it requiring wall protection even in Southern England. The leaves are deep green and pinnate, while the greenish-white flowers are fragrant, and produced in the beginning of summer. Soil warm and light.

S. LATIFOLIA. See HOLBŒLLIA.

Stephanandra (Rosaceæ).

STEPHANANDRA FLEXUOSA.—Japan. This is a desirable shrub of somewhat procumbent growth, with neatly-toothed leaves and producing an abundance of small white flowers. It grows well in peaty loam, and is deciduous.

S. TANAKÆ is not of equal floral beauty with the former, these being of a greenish tinge, while the leaves are of larger size.

Stuartia (Ternstromiaceæ).

STUARTIA PENTAGYNA (*syn Malachodendron ovatum*).—North America, 1785. This differs only from the S. virginica in having five distinct styles, hence the name. Under very favourable circumstances this is the taller growing species, and the leaves and flowers are larger. The leaves are oval and the flowers crimson coloured.

S. PSEUDO-CAMELLIA (*syn S. grandiflora*).—Japan, 1879. This differs from the others in the flowers being rather larger, 2 inches to 3 inches across, and of a purer white, and supplied with yellow instead of red stamens. The foliage tint in autumn is exceedingly showy. It is quite hardy in Southern England and Ireland at least.

S. VIRGINICA (*syn S. marylandica*).—North America, 1743. This is a handsome, free-growing shrub, of often 10 feet in height, with large, creamy-white flowers that are rendered all the more conspicuous by the crimson-red stamens. The flowers—like those of a single Rose, and fully 2½ inches across—are produced in May. Quite hardy, as many fine specimens in some of our old English gardens will point out.

Though, perhaps, rather exacting in their requirements, the Stuartias may be very successfully grown if planted in light, moist, peaty earth, and where they will be screened from cold, cutting winds.

Styphnolobium. See Sophora.

Styrax (Styraceæ).

STYRAX AMERICANA and S. PULVERULENTA are not commonly cultivated, being far less showy than the Japanese species. They bear white flowers.

S. OBASSIA.—Japan, 1888. A beautiful flowering species, with large, rounded leaves, which are often 8 inches across, the sweetly-scented white flowers being plentifully produced in drooping racemes. They are all readily cultivated.

S. OFFICINALIS.—Storax. Levant, 1597. This is a small, deciduous shrub, with ovate leaves, and short racemes of pretty pure-white flowers. A not very hardy species, and only second-rate as an ornamental flowering shrub.

S. SERRULATA VIRGATA (*syn S. japonica*).—Japanese Storax. Japan. A neat-habited and dense-growing shrub, with pretty white flowers that are neatly set off by the showy yellow stamens. It is an extremely pretty shrub, with long, slender, much-branched shoots, furnished with ovate leaves, and deliciously-scented, snow-white, bell-shaped flowers, produced for nearly the full length of the shoots. So far, this shrub of recent introduction has proved quite hardy. S. serrulata variegata is a well-marked and constant form. A light soil is necessary for their cultivation.

Symphoria. See Symphoricarpus.

Symphoricarpus (Caprifoliaceæ).

SYMPHORICARPUS OCCIDENTALIS.—Wolf Berry. North America. This species has larger and more freely produced pinky-white flowers and smaller fruit than the commonly cultivated plant.

S. RACEMOSUS (*syn Symphoria racemosus*).—Snowberry. North America, 1817. One of the commonest shrubs in English gardens, with small, oval, entire leaves, and neat little racemes of pretty pink flowers, succeeded by the familiar snow-white berries, and for which the shrub is so remarkable.

S. VULGARIS.—Coral Berry, Common St. Peter's Wort. North America, 1730. This is readily distinguished by its small red and yellow flowers, and freely produced coral berries. There is a very neat and much-sought-after variety, having conspicuous green and yellow leaves, and named S. vulgaris foliis variegatis.

The Snowberries are of no great value as ornamental shrubs, but owing to their succeeding well in the very poorest and stoniest of soils, and beneath the shade and drip of trees, are to be recommended for cultivation. They grow and spread freely, and are therefore useful where unchecked and rampant shrub growth is desirable.

Symplocos (Styracaceæ).

SYMPLOCOS JAPONICA (*syn S. lucida*). A small-growing and not very desirable species from Japan (1850), with pale-yellow flowers and obovate-elliptic leaves which are 2 inches long.

S. TINCTORIA.—Sweet-leaf, or Horse Sugar. South United States, 1780. This is a small-growing shrub, with clusters of fragrant yellow flowers, and leaves 4 inches to 5 inches long. It is not very hardy unless planted against a sheltered and sunny wall.

Syringa (Oleaceæ).

SYRINGA CHINENSIS (*syns S. dubia* and *S. rothomagensis*). —Rouen, or Chinese Lilac. A plant of small growth, with narrow leaves and reddish-violet flowers. It is said to have been raised by M. Varin, of the Botanic Garden, Rouen, as a hybrid between S. vulgaris and S. persica, 1795.

S. Emodi.—Himalayas, 1840. This is a desirable species, that forms a stout bush or small tree, with oblong, reticulately-veined leaves, and erect, dense panicles of white flowers that are sometimes lilac tinged. The flowers are strongly scented, and borne in great profusion late in the season. There is a variegated form, S. Emodi variegata, and another named S. Emodi villosa, both good varieties.

S. japonica (*syns S. amurensis* and *Ligustrina amurensis*).—Japan. This is of recent introduction, and is a decided acquisition, producing in summer large and dense clusters of creamy-white flowers. It is a very desirable species, and though coming from Japan seems to be perfectly hardy.

S. Josikæa, Josika's Lilac, is of Hungarian origin (1835), and is so totally different from the others as to be well worthy of special attention. It rarely exceeds 6 feet in height, with dark-green, wrinkled leaves, and erect spikes of pale-mauve flowers.

S. persica.—Persian Lilac. Persia, 1640. This is a distinct small-growing species, with slender, straight branches, and lilac or white flowers produced in small clusters. The form bearing white flowers is named S. persica alba; and there is one with neatly divided foliage called S. persica laciniata.

S. vulgaris.—Common Lilac, or Pipe Tree. Persia and Hungary, 1597. This is one of the commonest and most highly praised of English garden shrubs, and one that has given rise, either by natural variation or by crossing with other species, to a great number of superior forms. The following include the best and most ornamental of the numerous varieties: alba, pure-white flowers; alba-grandiflora, very large clusters of white flowers; alba-magna, and alba virginalis, both good white-flowering forms; Dr. Lindley, large clusters of reddish-lilac flowers; Charles X., purplish-lilac flowers, but white when forced; Souvenir De Ludwig Spath, with massive clusters of richly coloured flowers; Glorie de Moulins, Marie Legrange, Noisetteana, Duchesse de Nemours, and Vallettiana, all beautiful flowering forms that are well worthy of cultivation, and of the simplest growth.

The double-flowered varieties, for which we are much indebted to M. Victor Lemoine, of Nancy, are fast gaining favour with cultivators in this country, and rightly, too, for they include several very handsome, full flowered forms. The following are best known :—

S. vulgaris Alphonse Lavallee, with full double red flowers, changing to mauve.
,, Charles Joly, dark red.
,, Condorcet, blue and white.
,, Dr. Masters, lilac.
,, Emile Lemoine, mauve-pink, suffused with white; very handsome.
,, La Tour d'Auvergne, mauve shaded with rose. A beautiful and very dark coloured form.
,, Lemoinei, nearly resembling our common species, but with full double flowers.
,, Leon Simon, light pink, mauve shaded.
,, Madame Lemoine, the finest form, bearing very large pure-white double flowers.
,, Michael Buchner, rosy lilac.
,, President-Carnot, pale lilac, white centres.
,, Virginité, whitish pink, nearly white when fully expanded.

President Grevy is one of the same beautiful group. The blooms are large, double, and produced in very massive clusters, and of a light bluish-lilac tint, when forced almost white. The first of this group, S. vulgaris Lemoinei, was sent out about 1884, and was then awarded a certificate by the Royal Horticultural Society. The range in colouring of these Lilacs is rather confined, so that the various forms resemble one another in no small degree, particularly when the flowers are opened under glass. From the large size of the flower bunches, and the individual flowers being double, they are all of great beauty, and being quite hardy still further enhances their value for outdoor gardening purposes.

The Lilacs grow freely in any soil of fair quality, but a free, rich, and not too dry loam, would seem to suit the majority of these plants best.

The Philadelphus or Mock Orange is frequently but erroneously called Syringa.

Tamarix (Tamariscineæ).

TAMARIX GALLICA (*syn T. anglica*).—Common Tamarisk. India to Europe. This shrub often in favoured maritime places reaches to a height of fully 10 feet, with long and slender branches, and spikes of pretty, rosy-pink flowers produced at the end of summer. For seaside planting, it is an invaluable shrub, and on account of its feathery appearance and wealth of showy flowers is well worthy of being included in our list of ornamental and useful shrubs.

T. PARVIFLORA (*syns T. africana* and *T. tetrandra*), South-Eastern Europe and Levant, is nearly allied to T. gallica, with white, pinky-tinged flowers. Other species are T. chinensis, a graceful, hardy shrub, with long spikes of pink flowers; and T. Odessana (Odessa, 1891), with reddish bark and compound racemes of flowers.

The Tamarisks thrive best in sandy soil and a maritime situation.

Tasmannia. See Drimys.

Tecoma (Bignoniaceæ).

TECOMA GRANDIFLORA (*syn Bignonia grandiflora*), from China and Japan (1800), is not so hardy as T. radicans, although in certain maritime districts it succeeds fairly well. The flowers are very attractive, being of a rich orange-scarlet, and produced in drooping clusters. Both foliage and flowers are larger than those of T. radicans. It wants a warm, sunny wall, and light, rich, well-drained soil, and if only for the lovely flowers it is well worthy of coddling and good treatment.

T. RADICANS (*syn Bignonia radicans*).—Trumpet Flower. North America, 1640. An old occupant of our gardens and one of the most beautiful wall plants in cultivation. It is a tall climber, of sometimes fully 20 feet in height, with graceful pinnate leaves, and handsome trumpet-shaped scarlet-red flowers that are at their best about mid-summer, though the period of flowering extends over a considerable length of time. The stems are long, twisted, and wiry, and like those of the Ivy send out roots at the joints and so fasten the plant in position. Few climbing plants are more attractive than the Trumpet Flower, and being hardy in most parts of the country, and free of growth, is to be recommended for covering walls and arches, or similar structures. T. radicans major is of more robust growth than the species, with larger foliage and paler flowers. The orange-scarlet flowers are produced in terminal corymbs. Any well-drained loam will suit the Tecoma.

Teucrium (Labiateæ).

TEUCRIUM FRUTICANS.—South Europe, 1869. This is an evergreen shrub, about a yard in height, with entire, ovate leaves that are rufescent beneath, and blue flowers. It requires a sheltered site and good garden loam.

Thermopsis. See Piptanthus.

Tilia (Tiliaceæ).

TILIA VULGARIS (*syns T. europæa* and *T. intermedia*).—Lime, or Linden Tree. Europe, Caucasus, and naturalised in Britain. Probably none of the Limes would be included in a list of ornamental flowering trees and shrubs, still that they are of great interest and beauty even in that state cannot be denied. The common species as well as its numerous varieties have sweetly-scented, yellowish-white flowers in terminal cymes, and are, though individually small, highly ornamental when fully developed. Other species of great interest when in flower are T. alba (*syn T. argentea*), Silver Lime (Eastern Europe, 1767); T. petiolaris, a curious and beautiful species; and T. euchlora.

The various species and varieties of Lime succeed well in almost any class of soil, but rich loam on sand is considered the most suitable for their perfect development.

Trachelospermum (Apocynaceæ).

TRACHELOSPERMUM JASMINOIDES (*syn Rhynchospermum jasminoides*).—Japan. This is a half-hardy climbing shrub, with glossy-green leaves and a plentiful supply of white, sweet-scented flowers at midsummer. In the South of England and Ireland it has proved quite hardy, but northwards it suffers from frost and long-continued cold winds. It is an interesting creeper which fastens itself to a wall or building by aerial roots somewhat after the fashion of the common Ivy. Very good soil would seem to suit it.

Trochodendron (Magnoliaceæ).

Trochodendron araliodes.—Japan (1894, or before). A distinct small-growing tree with large evergreen leaves that vary from 4 inches to 5 inches in length and, when well established, bearing both flowers and fruit in this country. The flowers are green and star-like in shape. We have found it somewhat difficult to deal with, but in several parts of England, the warmer and more sheltered, it has become quite established.

Ulex (Leguminoseæ).

Ulex europæus.—Furze, Gorse, or Whin. This pretty native shrub needs no description, suffice it to say that it is one of the handsomest flowering species in cultivation. U. europæus flore-pleno (Double-flowered Gorse) is even more beautiful than the species, the wealth of golden flowers almost hiding the plant from view. U. europæus strictus (Irish Furze) is of more erect and slender growth, and less rigid than the common species.

U. nanus.—Dwarf Gorse, Cat Whin, and Tam Furze. This differs considerably from the common plant, not only in stature, but in the time of flowering. In this species the bracts at the calyx base are small compared with those of U. europæus, while the smaller flowers are produced during summer, and when not a bloom is to be found on its supposed parent. It is of dense growth, the tallest stems rarely rising from the ground to a greater height than about 15 inches.

All the Furze family succeed admirably in the poorest of soil; indeed, a dry gravelly bank would seem to be their favourite haunt.

Vaccinium (Vacciniaceæ).

Vaccinium corymbosum. — Canada to Carolina and Georgia, 1765. This is one of the most beautiful and showy species, with dense clusters of small, pinky flowers.

V. Erythrocarpum.—A branching shrub, about a yard high, with deciduous leaves, flesh-coloured flowers, and dark-red fruit.

V. Myrtillus.—Whortleberry, Bilberry, Blackberry, and Blueberry. A native plant, with angular stems, ovate-toothed leaves, and pinky-white flowers, succeeded by bright, bluish-black berries.

P. pennsylvanicum.—New England to Virginia, 1772. This has rather inconspicuous flowers, and is of greatest value for the autumnal foliage tints.

V. Vitis-Idea (Cowberry, Flowering Box, or Brawlins), a native species, has racemose flowers and red berries.

Other species that might be included are V. canadense, V. stamineum, V. frondosum, V. ligustrifolium, and V. hirsutum, the latter remarkable for the brick-red colour of the whole plant in autumn.

The various species of Vaccinium are of dwarf or procumbent growth, and only suitable for planting in beds, or on rockwork, where they will not be lost sight of. They thrive best in soil of a peaty nature.

Verbena. See Lippia.

Veronica (Scrophularineæ).

Veronica pinguifolia.—New Zealand, 1870. This is one of the hardiest species, but it is of low growth, and only suitable for alpine gardening. It is a dwarf spreading shrub, with intensely glaucous leaves and white flowers.

V. Traversii.—New Zealand, 1873. This may be considered as one of the few species of hardy Veronicas. It grows about 4 feet high, with deep-green leaves arranged in rows, and white flowers, produced late in summer. It is a very free-growing shrub, of perfect hardihood, and one of, if not the best for general planting.

The above two species are, so far as is at present known, the hardiest in cultivation, although there are many kinds that will succeed well under very favourable conditions, and particularly when planted by the seaside. Other half-hardy species might include V. salicifolia (Willow-leaved Veronica), with long, narrow leaves, and white or purplish flowers; V. ligustrifolia (Privet-leaved Veronica), with spikes of feathery-white flowers; V. speciosa, with erect spikes of purplish-blue flowers; and V. Andersoni, a hybrid form, with spikes of bluish-violet flowers. V. hulkeana is another desirable species.

The dwarf or alpine species might include V. cupressoides, with Cypress-like foliage, V. Lyallii, V. carnosula, and others, but such hardly come within our scope.

The Veronicas thrive best in light, loamy soil.

Viburnum (Caprifoliaceæ)

Viburnum acerifolium.—Dockmackie. New England to Carolina, 1736. This is one of the handsomest members of the family, being of slender growth and compact and neat in habit. It grows to fully 4 feet in height, and is well supplied with neatly three-lobed leaves, these in the autumn turning to a deep crimson. The white or yellowish-white flowers, too, are highly ornamental, being borne in fair-sized clusters. It is a very desirable and beautiful plant, quite hardy, and of free growth in any fairly rich soil.

V. Awafukii.—Japan, 1842. This is another rare and beautiful plant, of neat habit, and bearing an abundance of showy white flowers, that are, however, seldom produced in this country.

V. Carlesii.—Corea, 1902. This is a recently introduced species with ovate leaves upwards of 2 inches long, with toothed margins, and covered on both surfaces with a soft pubescence. The flowers, which are produced in May, are of a leathery texture, white inside, but pink on the outer surface, and deliciously perfumed. In peat and loam it thrives at Kew, and in a fully exposed situation.

V. CASSINOIDES (*syn V. pyrifolium*).—North America, 1761, is a swamp-loving species, with thick, coriaceous leaves 2 inches long, and flat cymes of white or yellowish-white flowers.

V. DAHURICUM.—Dahuria, 1785. This is a charming hardy species, which in May and June is covered with numerous umbels of showy white flowers. It forms a rather spreading bush 6 feet or 8 feet high, with grey downy branches and neat foliage. The berries are oval-oblong, red at first, but becoming black and faintly scented when fully ripe.

V. DENTATUM.—Arrowwood. A native of the United States, 1763. This can be recommended as a distinct and beautiful shrub, with cymes of white flowers that are produced in plenty. The leaves are dark green, smooth, and shining, and strongly veined, while the bark is ash-coloured, and the berries bright blue.

V. FURCATUM.—Japan. This species has unusually large leaves, which assume a scarlet tint in autumn.

V. LANTANA.—Wayfaring Tree. Europe (Britain). This is a native species of large bush, or almost tree growth, with rugose, oblong, serrulated leaves, and large, flat cymes of white flowers appearing in May and June. The whole tree is usually covered with a scaly tomentum, while the fruit is a black flattened drupe.

V. LENTAGO.—Sheepberry and Sweet Viburnum. North America, 1761. This resembles our native V. Lantana, with dense clusters of white blossoms succeeded by black berries.

V. MACROCEPHALUM (*syn V. Fortunei*).—China, 1844. This is a beautiful species, but one that cannot be depended on as hardy enough to withstand our most severe winters. It has very large heads or panicles of white neutral flowers. Against a sunny wall and in a cosy nook it may occasionally be found doing fairly well, but it is not to be generally recommended.

V. Nudum.—American Withe Rod. Canada to Georgia, 1752. This is also worthy of being included in a selection of these shrubs.

V. Opulus.—Guelder Rose. A native shrub of great beauty, whether in foliage, flower, or fruit. The leaves are variously lobed or deeply toothed, large and handsome, and the flower heads of good size, flat, and composed of a number of small flowers, the outer only being sterile. Individually the flowers are dull and inconspicuous, but being produced in amazing quantity they have a very pleasing and effective appearance. The great bunches of clear pinky berries render a fair-sized plant particularly handsome and attractive, and for which alone, as also beauty of autumnal foliage, the shrub is well worthy of extensive culture. It grows fully 15 feet high, and may frequently be seen as much through. V. Opulus sterilis (Snowball Tree) is one of the commonest occupants of our shrubberies, and a decidedly ornamental flowering shrub. The large, almost globular flower heads hanging from every branch tip are too well known to require description, and have made the shrub one of the most popular in ornamental planting.

V. pauciflorum is a native of cold, moist woods from Labrador to Alaska, and may best be described as a miniature V. Opulus. It rarely grows more than 4 feet high, with small cymes of flowers, that are devoid of the neutral flowers of that species.

V. plicatum, from Japan, 1846, is another very beautiful and desirable shrub, of rather dwarf, spreading growth, and having the leaves deeply wrinkled, plaited, and serrated on the margins. The flowers resemble those of the commonly cultivated species, but they are rather larger, and of a purer white. It is a decidedly ornamental shrub, of easy growth in any good soil and where not exposed to cold winds. This has been referred to as V. tomentosum by some writers.

V. PRUNIFOLIUM, New England to Carolina, 1731, with Plum-like leaves, and pretty white flowers, is another free-growing and beautiful North American species.

V. PYRIFOLIUM.—Pear-leaved Viburnum. Pennsylvania to New Jersey, 1812. This is a rarely seen, but very ornamental species, with oval-shaped, finely-toothed leaves that are borne on short, slightly-winged stalks about half an inch long. Flowers sweetly scented, white, and in broad corymbs, the feathery appearance of the long, projecting stamens, each tipped with a golden anther, adding considerably to the beauty of the flowers.

V. RHYTIDOPHYLLUM.—This is a new Wayfaring Tree, which has been introduced by Messrs. J. Veitch and Sons, Chelsea, from China. It is of bold habit of growth with large leaves entirely different from anything we have seen before. They are opposite, oblong, 4 inches to 8 inches in length, and 2 inches to 3 inches in width, very much wrinkled, dark green and shining above. The under-surface is covered with a rusty grey tomentum. The flowers are produced in large flattened bunches terminating the stems and give rise to berries that are first red, then black and shining. A plant about 7 feet high and 6 feet wide was shown by the above firm, and received a first-class certificate from the Royal Horticultural Society.

V. SIEBOLDI (*syn V. reticulatum*), from Japan, is a worthy species with opposite dark-green leaves and freely-produced flowers.

V. TINUS.—Laurustinus. South Europe, 1596. So commonly cultivated a shrub needs no description here, sufficient to say that the handsome evergreen foliage and pretty pinky-white flowers assign to it a first position amongst hardy ornamental flowering shrubs. V. Tinus strictum has darker foliage than the species, is more upright, rather more hardy, but not so profuse in the bearing of flowers. V. Tinus lucidum (Glossy-leaved Laurustinus), of the several varieties of Laurustinus, has the largest foliage, finest flowers, and altogether is of the most robust growth. It is, unfortunately, not very hardy, probably in that respect not even equalling the parent plant. Usually it does not flower freely, neither are the flowers produced so early as in the species, but individually they are much larger. It is of tall growth, and rarely forms the neat dense bush, for which the common shrub is so admired. V. Tinus rotundifolium has rounded leaves; and V. Tinus rotundifolium variegatum has irregularly variegated leaves.

V. TOMENTOSUM MARIESI is a very floriferous and desirable variety of the less beautiful species V. tomentosum with cream-white, sterile flowers.

V. UTILE (China, 1880) is another desirable new species that would appear to be perfectly hardy in this country.

Any free, loamy soil will suit their wants.

Vinca (Apocyneæ).

VINCA MAJOR.—Band-plant, Cut-finger, and Larger Periwinkle. Europe (Britain). For trailing over tree-stumps or rockwork this pretty evergreen shrub has a distinctive value, the bright-green leaves and showy deep-blue flowers rendering it both conspicuous and ornamental. V. major elegantissima is a decided variety, the leaves being neatly and evenly variegated, and making the plant of great value for bank or rockwork decoration, while V. major alba has white flowers.

V. MINOR.—Lesser Periwinkle. This is of much smaller growth than the preceding, and differs, too, in not having the leaf-margins ciliated. The variety V. minor flore-albo has white flowers, those of the normal plant being pale blue; V. minor flore-pleno differs in having double blue flowers; V. minor foliis aureis has golden-tinted leaves; and V. minor foliis argenteis bears silvery mottled and very attractive foliage.

They are all of simple growth, succeeding well in somewhat shady situations, and in by no means the richest of soil. As they run about freely and soon cover an extent of ground they are rendered of great value for a variety of purposes.

Vitex (Verbenaceæ).

VITEX AGNUS-CASTUS.—Chaste Tree, Hemp Tree, and Monk's Pepper-tree. A South European shrub (1670), growing from 6 feet to 10 feet high, with digitate leaves that are almost hoary beneath, and spikes of small violet flowers. It is not very hardy, although in some of the warmer parts of Southern England and Ireland, fair-sized, healthy-looking specimens are now and then to be met with. As a wall plant, however, it succeeds best, and for which purpose, with its neat foliage and pretty flowers, it is peculiarly suitable.

Vitis (Ampelideæ).

VITIS HETEROPHYLLA HUMILIFOLIA.—Turquoise-berried Vine. North China and Japan, 1868. The leaves of this Vine are three to five lobed, and the small flowers freely produced in slightly branching cymes. The latter are succeeded by their most interesting and attractive berries, that ripen in September and October. They are pale china-blue, marked all over with very dark specks. The stems grow to a height of 4 feet to 8 feet, and should be trained against a wall in a sunny position to ripen the berries. The plant is perfectly hardy. The variety V.

heterophylla variegata is a dwarf, low-growing plant with variegated leaves, and is used for pot work, for covering the ground in sub-tropical bedding designs, and might be used to great advantage for rambling over large stones in the rock garden. V. Coignetiæ and V. Thunbergii, though not remarkable for beauty of flowers, are highly valued for the brilliant shades of their autumn foliage.

Weigela. See Diervilla.

Wistaria (Leguminoseæ).

WISTARIA CHINENSIS (*syns W. sinensis, Glycine chinensis,* and *G. sinensis*).—Chinese Wistaria. China, 1816. This is the only species at all common in gardens, and by far the handsomest in cultivation. It justly ranks amongst the most beautiful of hardy climbing shrubs, and is invaluable as a wall plant, or for clothing the bare stems of sparsely foliaged trees. The purplish-lilac flowers are produced in long, drooping racemes in early summer. W. chinensis alba has pretty white flowers; W. chinensis flore-pleno has not proved very satisfactory, but when seen at its best, which is, however, but rarely, the double flowers are both beautiful and showy; W. chinensis variegata has badly variegated foliage; and W. chinensis macrobotrya is a plant of great beauty with very long racemes of pale-lavender flowers, but they vary a good deal in colour, those of some plants being almost white. It is a very desirable variety, and one that when better known is sure to attract attention.

W. FRUTESCENS (*syns Glycine frutescens* and *Thyrsanthus frutescens*).—North America, 1724. This is a very handsome deciduous climbing species from North America. The flowers, which appear towards autumn, are bluish-purple and fragrant, and borne in erect racemes. It is quite hardy and equally suitable with the Chinese species for using as a wall-covering. W. frutescens magnifica is an improved form of the species; while W. frutescens alba has white flowers, and W. frutescens purpurea purple flowers.

W. JAPONICA.—Japan. A bush-like species bearing white flowers, but it is rarely seen in cultivation. It is, however, quite hardy, and succeeds well in the bush state at Kew.

W. MULTIJUGA.—Japan, 1874. Resembles somewhat our commonly cultivated species, and has pale-purple flowers arranged in long racemes. It is a very ornamental and desirable species, but the flowers are not borne in great quantity.

The Wistarias are of simple culture, but succeed best in rather rich alluvial soil, and where protection from cold winds is provided. They are of slow growth for several years after being planted.

Xanthoceras (Sapindaceæ).

XANTHOCERAS SORBIFOLIA.—China, 1870. An extremely pretty flowered and handsome leaved shrub. So far it has proved itself perfectly hardy in this country, there being specimens at wide distances apart that have stood uninjured through many severe winters.

The leaves are pale green, and pinnate, somewhat resembling those of the Rowan Tree. Flowers five-petalled, creamy-white, sometimes very slightly tinged with flesh colour, with a coppery red or violet-purple centre, and disposed in racemes. When fully expanded they are an inch across, and somewhat reflexed. It flowers early in April, with the appearance of the leaves, the blooms being produced in great abundance, in spike-like clusters fully 7 inches long, and succeeded by a small green Pear-like fruit. This is one of the most distinct and handsome of recently introduced shrubs, and will, when more widely disseminated, be largely planted for purely ornamental purposes. It grows from 10 feet to about 15 feet high.

Xanthorhiza (Ranunculaceæ).

Xanthorhiza apiifolia.—Yellow-root. Pennsylvania, 1776. A small-growing shrub, with yellow creeping roots, from which suckers are thrown up profusely. The leaves are irregularly pinnate, and the minute flowers, which are borne in large, branching spikes, are of a peculiar dark-purple colour. It prefers a cool, moist situation.

Xylosteum. See Lonicera.

Yucca (Liliaceæ).

Yucca elata.—United States, 1893. This has pale-green leaves about 2 feet long, and sweetly-scented white flowers in a dense panicle. It grows about 10 feet high.

Y. filamentosa.—Silk Grass. North America, 1675. A well-known and beautiful plant, with numerous leaves arranged in a dense rosette, and from 1 foot to 2 feet long by 2 inches broad. Flower scape rising to 5 feet or 6 feet in height, and bearing numerous flowers that are each about 2 inches deep. There is a beautiful variegated form of this species named Y. filamentosa variegata, and one with much narrower leaves than the typical species, and known as Y. filamentosa angustifolia.

Y. gloriosa.—The Mound Lily. United States, 1596. This is another well-known hardy species, with long, sharp-pointed leaves, and a handsome, much-branched scape of flowers that are each about 2 inches deep. There are several varieties, differing in colour of foliage, including Y. gloriosa glaucescens, with decidedly glaucous foliage; Y. gloriosa superba, with rigid leaves and a shorter and denser flower scape; and another with variegated leaves. Y. gloriosa recurvifolia is usually dwarfer in the stem than the type, more inclined to branch than the other species, and less rigid, with recurving leaves that are not so sharp-pointed. The flower panicle is large and very much branched.

The Yuccas all do well if planted in light loam of good quality.

Zauschneria (Onagrarieæ).

ZAUSCHNERIA CALIFORNICA.—Californian Fuchsia, or Humming Birds' Trumpet. California and Mexico, 1847. A small-growing, densely-branched shrub, with linear-lanceolate silvery pubescent leaves, and bright-red or scarlet tubular flowers, with a long, slender style resembling some of the Fuchsias, and produced in September and October. It is a pretty and distinct Alpine shrub, and not being perfectly hardy should be assigned a rather warm and sheltered position.

Zelkova (Ulmaceæ).

ZELKOVA ACUMINATA (*syns Z. japonica, Z. kaki,* and *Planera acuminata*).—Japan, about 1872. This resembles very nearly our common Elm in appearance, and being perfectly hardy is to be recommended for planting in this country.

Z. CRENATA (*syns Planera crenata* and *P. Richardi*).—Zelkova Tree. Western Asia to Mount Caucasus, 1760. This is a handsome, large-growing tree, with oblong, deeply-crenated leaves and small and inconspicuous greenish, scented flowers. For avenue planting or as a standard specimen this is a valuable tree, being quite hardy, and of free and quick growth. Z. crenata pendula is a good weeping form, and worthy of culture.

Z. CRETICA.—Crete. A pretty small-growing bush or tree, about 20 feet in height, with crenate, leathery, dark-green leaves, which are usually fully an inch in length. The leaves are hairy, and the twigs, too, are thickly covered with short grey hairs. Light rich loam.

Zenobia (Ericaceæ).

ZENOBIA SPECIOSA (*syns Andromeda speciosa* and *A. cassinæfolia*).—South United States, 1800. This is one of the most distinct and pretty of hardy shrubs, and a native of damp low-lying districts. It grows about 4 feet high, and bears large pure-white, bell-shaped, Lily-of-the-Valley-like flowers in great abundance during the summer. In too dry situations it becomes sparse of foliage and unhappy, but grows and flowers freely in light, peaty soil. Z. speciosa pulverulenta is a very desirable variety, the whole plant—stems, foliage, and flowers—being of a pleasing light grey or white colour. Individually the flowers are larger than those of the species.

Planting a Shrub Group.

Where any defined system of shrub planting is attempted, it is usual to place the taller growing kinds in the centre or at the background and the dwarfer along the margin. Generally speaking, this is the correct method if the planting be not carried out in too formal a manner, but from the standpoint of natural arrangement such grouping is not strictly correct. Better it is to plant here and there through the mass taller shrubs of lithe and graceful habit, such as the Tamarisk and some of the Berberis, and Spiræas, avoiding sharp contrasts in their immediate vicinity. When the group or shrubbery is of large size, good masses of the same kind may be placed well back, but nearer the margin numerous varieties may be disposed. Due attention must, of course, be given to the arrangement of colours, and to the seasons of flowering.

To group shrubs so that they may have a natural and informal appearance is by no means easily accomplished, and the usual system of making circular or oval masses with the tallest in the centre and the smaller growing around the margin is too productive of extreme regularity and stiffness to be pleasing to the eye or generally adopted.

Where practicable, masses of each plant are preferable to single specimens, and the following lend themselves well to this style of planting:—

Rhus cotinus and R. typhina are both excellent when planted in masses in large beds or shrubberies, whether for beauty and quaintness of flowers, or the bright tints assumed by the autumn foliage.

Forsythia viridissima has few equals for planting in good bold masses, particularly alongside shrubs of a more sombre foliage colouring. Too sharp foliage contrasts should, however, be avoided, such as planting the purple-leaved plum and golden privet in close proximity. All the Brooms are good for the same purpose, so are the Lilacs, the many beautiful flowered Azaleas, the Daphnes, various species of Berberis, Cornus, Hippophæ or Sea Buckthorn, Deutzia, and various species of Viburnum. As a rule, planting should be carried out in autumn or early spring—the former time being preferable.

Pruning Flowering Shrubs.

Generally speaking, shrubs are pruned as a matter of course and with little or no consideration whether they will be benefited by the operation. While symmetry and regularity of outline are to be admired in a shrub, still such should never be gained at the expense of natural grace and production of flowers. The judicious pruner will, therefore, aim at preserving the habit peculiarity of each shrub as far as possible while interfering as little as can be avoided with the production of flowers. The various species of Deutzia, Forsythia, Philadelphus, and Weigelia flower on the wood of the preceding year's growth, therefore such shrubs should be pruned immediately after the flowering season—say in June, but never in spring or winter—at least, if the production of flowers is to be taken into account. Again, the various species of Syringa, Spiræa, Lonicera, and Hibiscus may safely be pruned during winter, the flowers being produced on the young wood, while Hydrangea paniculata grandiflora must be severely pruned back in early spring, for only by doing so will the greatest wealth of flowers be produced. Chimonanthus fragrans should be pruned in February; while the various species of Ceanothus should not be touched till all danger of frost is past. With the favourite Kerria japonica, pruning should be done in autumn, when old wood may be cut away. Pruning should be carefully carried out with a sharp knife, and not with the pruning shears, the point of amputation always taking place close to an eye or bud. Too severe pruning should always be avoided, a judicious thinning out of the branches being far preferable to indiscriminate shearing and cutting back.

Golden-leaved Trees and Shrubs.

These are particularly valuable for grouping with others of a dark-green colour, to which they impart a bright and cheerful appearance. The following are some of the best:—

Acacia Pseud-Acacia aurea
Catalpa bignonioides aurea
Corylus avellana aurea
Laburnum, golden
Philadelphus Gordoniana aurea
Privet, golden
Ptelia trifoliata, golden form
Ribes alpinum aureum
Sambucus nigra aurea
Spiræa opulifolia aurea
Weigelia Looymansii aurea

Trees and Shrubs with Autumn-tinted Foliage.

Acer palmatum atropurpureum
 sanguineum
Amelanchier canadensis
Ampelopsis japonica
Amygdalus persica purpurea
Andromeda arborea
Azalea pontica
Berberis Thunbergii
 vulgaris atropurpurea
Catalpa bignonioides aurea
Cerasus avium
Cornus florida
 alba Spathi
Cotoneaster Simonsii
Euonymus atropurpureus
 latifolia
Kolreuteria paniculata
Mahonia aquifolia
Parrotia persica
Rhus cotinoides
 cotinus
 glabra
 typhina
Ribes missouriense
Stephanandra flexuosa
Vaccinium of sorts
Viburnum opulus
 pauciflorum

Climbing and Wall Shrubs.

The list of shrubs that have been found suitable for covering walls or buildings would include—

Actinidia japonica
Akebia quinata
Ampelopsis, of sorts
Aristolochia sipho
Azara microphylla
Berberidopsis corallina
Berberis Darwinii
Bignonia radicans
Bridgesia spicata
Caprifolium (many varieties)
Ceanothus ,, ,,
Clematis ,, ,,
Cratægus pyracantha
Cydonia
Edwardsia microphylla
Escallonia, various
Garrya elliptica
Jasminum, of sorts
Kadsura
Lycium
Menispermum canadense
Passiflora, of sorts
Periploca græca
Roses, of sorts
Smilax
Wistaria

Berry-bearing Trees and Shrubs.

By the end of September the list of flowering shrubs is well-nigh exhausted, and attention is directed to the beauty and variety that is to be found amongst fruit-bearing subjects. In the following list will be found a selection of the best and most useful:—

Arbutus Unedo
Aucuba japonica
Berberis Darwinii
 vulgaris
 Wallichiana
Cotoneaster bacillaris
 buxifolia
 frigida
 rupestris
 Simonsii
Cratægus Aronia
 coccinea
 Crus-galli
 tanacetifolia
Daphne Mezereon
 alba
Elæagnus longipes
Eugenia Ugnii
Euonymus europæus
Euonymus latifolia
Gaultheria shallon
Hippophæ rhamnoides
Hymananthera crassifolia
Pernettya, many beautiful varieties
Pyrus Aria
 aucuparia
 Malus, in variety
Sambucus racemosus
Skimmia japonica
 oblata
Staphylea, several
Viburnum Opulus
Rosa cinnamomea
 pomifera
 rugosa
 spinosissima
 villosa

Winter Flowering Shrubs.

From November to March the following shrubs appear in flower, and are, therefore, rendered of particular value :—

Berberis Nepalensis
Chimonanthus fragrans
Cornus Mas
Corylopsis pauciflora
  spicata
Cratægus Oxyacantha præcox
Daphne Mezereum and varieties
Erica carnea
  codonodes
Hamamelis arborea
Hamamelis Japonica
  Zuccariniana
Jasminum nudiflorum
Lonicera fragrantissima
Rhododendron Nobleanum
  præcox
Prunus Amygdalus
Stachyurus præcox
Viburnum Tinus

Shrubs for the Shade.

The list of shrubs that will succeed well when planted beneath the shade and drip of trees is comparatively a short one, and would include the Periwinkles (Vinca major and V. minor), the St. John's Wort (Hypericum calycinum), the Mezereons (Daphne Mezereum and D. laureola), and the Alexandrian laurel (Ruscus racemosus). Of course, the common Ivy and Euonymus are also at home in shady situations, but they hardly come within the scope of this book.

In order to give the newly-planted shrubs the best chance of succeeding it is well to substitute the poverized soil beneath the trees by fresh loam, which will greatly assist the shrubs to start away and take to their new and trying situation.

Shrubs for Peaty Soil.

Some of our handsomest flowering shrubs belong to the section known as American or peat-loving, and of these the following are, perhaps, the most desirable :—

Andromeda (Zenobia) cassinæfolia
  floribunda
Bryanthus erectus
Clethra alnifolia
  paniculata
Dabœcia polifolia

Enkianthus campanulatus
Erica, in variety
Fothergilla alnifolia
Gaultheria Shallon
Halesia tetraptera
Kalmia angustifolia
latifolia
myrtifolia
Ledum latifolium
Ledum palustre
Leucothæ, in variety
Polygala chamæbuxus
purpurea
Prinos glaber
Rhodora canadensis
Rhododendron, of sorts
Vaccinium, various
Zenobia speciosa

Trees Suitable for Planting in Towns.

Acer macrophylla
saccharinum
Æsculus Hippocastanum
rubicunda
Ailanthus glandulosa
Catalpa bignonioides
Cerasus (Prunus), nearly all
Cratægus Oxyacantha
flore-plena
tenacetifolia
Gleditschia triacanthos
Liriodendron tulipifera
Magnolia acuminata
glauca
Pyrus, of sorts
Robinia Pseud-acacia and its varieties
viscosa
Sophora japonica
Tilia, in variety

Shrubs for Town Planting.

Amelanchier, in variety
Arbutus Unedo
Berberis Aquifolium
vulgaris
Cistus ladaniferus
laurifolius
Colutea arborescens
Daphne Laureola
Mezereum
Deutzia crenata
gracilis
Forsythia suspensa
viridissima
Griselinia littoralis
Hibiscus syriacus
Hypericum calycinum
nepalense
Kœlreuteria paniculata
Leycesteria formosa
Philadelphus Gordonianus
Prunus nana
Pyrus japonica
Rhus Cotinus
Ribes aureum
sanguineum
Skimmia japonica
Spiræa, in variety
Syringa (nearly all)
Ulex europæus fl.-pl.
Viburnum Opulus
Weigelia rosea
Yucca gloriosa
recurva

Trees for the Seaside.

Acer campestre
    saccharinum
Arbutus Unedo
Ailanthus glandulosa
Æsculus Hippocastanum
    rubicunda
Catalpa bignonioides
Fraxinus Ornus

Shrubs for the Seaside.

Atriplex halimus
Buddleia globosa
Cerasus lusitanica
Choisya ternata
Cytisus Laburnum
    scoparius
Euonymus japonicus
    europæus
Fabiana imbricata
Griselinia littoralis
Hippophæ rhamnoides
Ilex Aquifolium
Laurus nobilis
Lycium europæum
Prunus Padus
Rhamnus frangula
Ribes sanguineum
Rosa spinosissima
Shepherdia argentea
Spiræa adiantifolia
Syringa persica
    vulgaris
Symphoricarpus racemosus
Tamarix gallica
    germanica
Ulex europæus
Veronica, in variety
Viburnum Tinus

Shrubs suitable for Hedges.

Berberis
Cytisus
Ligustrum
Prunus
Rhododendron
Rosa
Symphoricarpus
Syringa
Ulex
Viburnum

THE FLOWERING SEASONS OF TREES AND SHRUBS.

The asterisk (*) after the name denotes that the species continues in flower for a longer period than the month under which it is placed.

JANUARY.

Chimonanthus fragrans *
Cratægus Oxyacantha præcox *
Erica carnea *
Jasminum nudiflorum *
Ulex europæus *
Viburnum Tinus *

FEBRUARY.

Cornus Mas *
Daphne Laureola *
  Mezereum *
Hamamelis japonica
Lonicera fragrantissima *
Magnolia conspicua *
Parrotia persica *
Pittosporum Tobira *
Prunus nana *
  Davidiana *
Rosmarinus officinalis *

MARCH.

Arbutus Andrachne *
Berberis japonica *
Erica mediterranea *
Forsythia viridissima *
Garrya elliptica
Magnolia stellata *
Nuttallia cerasiformis *
Prunus Amygdalus *
  ilicifolia *
  japonica *
Prunus spinosa *
  triloba *
  tomentosa
Rhododendron dahuricum
  ledifolium
Skimmia Fortunei
Spiræa Thunbergi *
Xanthoriza apiifolia *

APRIL.

Akebia quinata *
Amelanchier alnifolia
  canadensis
  vulgaris
Berberis Aquifolium *
  Darwinii *
  pinnata
  vulgaris
Cæsalpinia sepiaria
Caragana frutescens
  spinosa *
Ceanothus cuneatus *
  rigidus *
Clematis cirrhosa *
  florida *
Cornus florida
Cytisus scoparius *
Daphne altaica
  Blagayana
  Cneorum *
  Genkwa
  sericea
Deutzia gracilis *
Diervilla rosea *

Drimys aromatica
Fothergilla alnifolia *
Fremontia californica
Halesia diptera
tetraptera
Kalmia glauca *
Laburnum vulgare *
Ledum latifolium
palustre
Lonicera Caprifolium *
tatarica *
Magnolia cordata *
Fraseri
Lennei
obovata discolor
Pieris floribunda *
japonica *
Prunus Avium Juliana
cerasifera
cerasifera Pissardii
Cerasus
domestica
divaricata
Mahaleb
maritima
Padus *
paniculata flore-pleno
Puddum *
sinensis
Pyrus angustifolia
baccata *
floribunda *
japonica Maulei
prunifolia *
rivularis *
sinica
vestita
Rhododendron campanulatum
Rhodora *
Rhodotypos kerrioides
Ribes aureum *
cereum
floridum *
sanguineum
Rosa indica *
Sambucus racemosa *
Skimmia japonica
Laureola
Spiræa prunifolia
Stuartia virginica *
Syringa Emodi
Xanthoceras sorbifolia

MAY.

Abelia triflora *
Æsculus glabra
Hippocastanum
Arbutus Menziesii
Berberis aristata *
Bealei
empetrifolia
sinensis
trifoliolata
Wallichiana
Calycanthus floridus *
Caragana arborescens
microphylla
Ceanothus dentatus *
Cercis canadensis
Siliquastrum
Chionanthus retusa
virginica
Citrus trifoliata
Cladrastis tinctoria
Clematis alpina *
montana *
Cornus canadensis
stolonifera
Coronilla Emerus *
Cratægus Azarolus
Azarolus Aronia
coccinea
cordata *
Crus-galli
Douglasii
Oxyacantha *
parvifolia
Pyracantha
tenacetifolia
Cytisus albus *
albus incarnatus *
biflorus *
Daphne alpina *
Deutzia crenata *
Epigæa repens
Exochorda grandiflora
Fabiana imbricata
Fraxinus Ornus *
Mariesii
Gaultheria Shallon
Genista lusitanica
pilosa *
prostrata *
Halesia parviflora
Halimodendron argenteum *
Laburnum Adami *

Leiophyllum buxifolium *
Leucothoë axillaris
Catesbæi
Magnolia acuminata *
glauca
Umbrella
Ostrya carpinifolia
Pæonia Moutan
Pernettya mucronata *
Philadelphus coronarius
Pieris Mariana *
ovalifolia
Pitpanthus nepalensis
Polygala Chamæbuxus *
Prunus Chamæcerasus
pennsylvanica
virginiana *
Pyrus Aria *
Aucuparia *
coronaria
germanica
prunifolia
sinensis
Smithii *
torminalis
Rhododendron arborescens
calendulaceum
Collettiana
ferrugineum *
flavum
hirsutum *
molle
ponticum
racemosum
Ribes speciosum
Robinia hispida
Pseud-Acacia *
viscosa
Rosa spinosissima *
Rubus biflorus
deliciosus
spectabilis *
Sophora tetraptera
Spiræa cantoniensis
lævigata
trilobata
Staphylea pinnata *
trifolia *
Stuartia pentagyna *
Syringa chinensis *
Josikæa
persica *
vulgaris *
Vaccinium corymbosum *
pennsylvanicum

Viburnum acerifolium *
Lantana *
Lentago *
nudum *
plicatum *
prunifolium
pyrifolium *
Wistaria chinensis *
multijuga *

JUNE.

Adenocarpus decorticans *
Æsculus californica *
Andromeda polifolia
Bryanthus erectus
Buddleia globosa *
Lindleyana *
paniculata *
Calophaca wolgarica *
Calycanthus occidentalis *
Carpenteria californica
Castanea sativa
Catalpa speciosa
Ceanothus azureus *
Choisya ternata *
Cistus crispus *
ladaniferus
laurifolius *
monspeliensis *
purpureus *
salvifolius *
Clematis lanuginosa *
patens *
Viorna
Viticella
Colutea arborescens *
cruenta *
Cornus circinata
macrophylla
Cratægus nigra *
Cytisus decumbens
nigricans
Daboëcia polifolia
Diervilla floribunda *
grandiflora *
Escallonia macrantha *
Fuchsia Riccartoni *
Genista ætnensis *
saggitalis
Helianthemum halimifolium *
lasianthum
lavendulæfolium *
pilosum *

Helianthemum polifolium *
umbellatum *
Hypericum calycinum *
patulum *
Itea virginica
Jamesia americana
Jasminum revolutum *
Kalmia angustifolia
latifolia *
Kerria japonica *
Laburnum alpinum
caramanicum
Ligustrum japonicum
lucidum *
ovalifolium *
sinense *
Liriodendron tulipifera *
Lyonia paniculata
Magnolia macrophylla
Myricaria germanica *
Myrtus communis *
Neillia opulifolia
Olearia macrodonta
Oxydendrum arboreum *
Philadelphus grandiflorus
hirsutus
inodorus
Lewisi
microphyllus *
Phlomis fruticosa
Plagianthus pulchellus *
Potentilla fruticosa
Prunus lusitanica
Rhododendron californicum
campylocarpum
chrysanthum
Rhus Cotinus *
Robinia dubia *
Rosa alba *
centifolia *
damascena *
gallica *
lutea
rubiginosa
rugosa
sempervirens *
Rubus arcticus
laciniatus *
odoratus *
Sambucus nigra
Spiræa bullata *
cana *
chamædrifolia *
decumbens *
hypericifolia *
Spiræa japonica *
media *
Staphylea colchica
Stuartia Pseudo-Camellia *
Syringa japonica *
Tecoma radicans *
Tilia vulgaris *
Veronica pinquifolia
Traversii *
Viburnum dahuricum *
dentatum
macrocephalum
Opulus *
Yucca filamentosa
Zenobia speciosa *

JULY.

Æsculus parviflora *
Berberis Fortunei
Ceanothus americanus *
Clematis Flammula *
Vitalba *
Cornus alba
alternifolia
tartarica
Escallonia floribunda
Phillipiana *
pterocladon
rubra *
Eucryphia pinnatifolia *
Fuchsia macrostema globosa
Genista anxanctica *
cinerea
germanica
hispanica *
radiata *
tinctoria *
Gordonia lasianthus *
Hydrangea hortensis *
Hypericum elatum
fasciculatum
hircinum *
prolificum *
uralum *
Jasminum fruticans *
humile *
Kalmia hirsuta *
Ligustrum Ibota *
Quihoi *
Lonicera Xylosteum *
Periploca græca *
Philadlephus Gordonianus
satzumi

Photinia arbutifolia
Plagianthus Lyalli
Philadelhpus Lemoinei
Rhododendron catawbiense
    maximum
    viscosum
Rosa bracteata
    hemisphærica
Spartium junceum *
Spiræa bella *
    discolor ariæfolia
    salicifolia *
    sorbifolia *
    tomentosa
Tamarix gallica *
    parviflora *
Tilia petiolaris *
Wistaria japonica *
Yucca gloriosa
Zauschneria californica

AUGUST.

Abelia chinensis *
Calluna vulgaris *
Catalpa bignonioides
Clerodendron fœtidum
Erica cinerea *
Escallonia illinita
Gordonia pubescens
Hedysarum multijugum
Hibiscus syriacus *
Hypericum oblongifolium
Leycesteria formosa *
Loropetalum chinense *
Magnolia grandiflora *
Nesæa salicifolia *
Passiflora cærulea *
Rubus nutkanus
Sophora japonica *
Spiræa Douglasii
    Lindleyana
Vitex Agnus-castus

SEPTEMBER.

Arbutus Unedo *
Baccharis halimifolia
Clerodendron trichotomum
Clethra acuminata *
    alnifolia
Daphne Cneorum *
Hydrangea paniculata grandiflora *
Olearia Haastii
    Gunniana
Photinia japonica
Microglossa albescens *
Tecoma grandiflora *

OCTOBER.

Berberidopsis corallina
Berberis nervosa *
Caryopteris Mastacanthus
Hamamelis virginica *
Lespedeza bicolor

NOVEMBER.

Azara microphylla
Cassinia fulvida
Chimonanthus fragrans *
Jasminum nudiflorum *

DECEMBER.

Chimonanthus fragrans *
Lardizabala biternata
Viburnum Tinus *

INDEX

Synonymous names are printed in italics.

THE END